BE IN BUSINESS

JACKY FITT

A creative collaboration with The Big Ideas Collective®.

All rights reserved.

ISBN: 978-1-7384604-0-3

First published in the United Kingdom, 2024 Big Ideas Library.

Design, Cartoons and Typeset by Ned Hoste of The Big Ideas Collective.

Printed in the UK by Mixam, Watford.

Best wishes
Jacky

Whoever we are and whatever we do, we all need our supporters and champions.

This book wouldn't be in front of you without the support, friendship and creative genius of Ned Hoste.

Thanks Ned.

**"If you want to go fast, go alone.
If you want to go far, go together."**
African Proverb.

A different kind of business startup guide.

Practical. Thoughtful. Human.

This book is all about you and how you can go from a good idea to a great business

Because going from a good idea to a profitable business is not quick, or particularly easy, but getting started in the right way can make a BIG difference to survival and ultimate success.

So why is this book different?

This book will form part of your 'tool kit'. Offering not just practical steps, it also focuses on your individual approach to risk and reward, decision making and good mental health. As my daughter says, "so it's about staying up when starting up" – yes it is. And more.

According to the World Bank, at the time of writing this, there are about 582 million and counting entrepreneurs on earth. Small businesses make up 90% of all companies and provide 50% of jobs worldwide. Half of those businesses started at home. BRIMCO 2023

If you are thinking of starting a business, or have already begun, this book offers a wealth of know-how, giving you, not just the best way to get going, but the right mindset to help you succeed.

Know yourself

Many people don't follow their dreams.

They don't believe they have what it takes to build their own business. They make excuses that prevent, them taking that leap of faith and many regret it. They may even try to sabotage another's efforts.

Generally, there are two types of people.

Those who are successful and those that can tell you all the reasons why they aren't.

"The person who says it cannot be done should not interrupt the person who is doing it."

Chinese Proverb.

Know your worth

We're going to stop self-doubt turning into self-sabotage, with the right mindset combined with great marketing; a practical and holistic approach to starting out and succeeding in business.

"... essential foundations from which to develop. The advice is timeless and applicable to business, career development and confidence building in arenas beyond the business world."

Chris Hiscocks, Enterprise Manager Biorenewables Development Centre

"A must read for anyone looking to start a business or who are in the early stages of their journey. Simple, practical and helps to remove a lot of the uncertainty around the HOW of starting a business."

Martin Johnson, Founder and CEO Trans2Performance

"What an amazing, truly authentic book for startups. The very practical sections along with space to reflect about the challenges of business are really helpful. Brilliant, I loved it as a very different approach from other books out there!"

Jackie Mathers PFHEA, Associate Pro Vice Chancellor CU Scarborough & CU Coventry, part of Coventry University Group

"Covering aspects from financial, to technical and relational, delivered in bite-sized chapters with space for your own notes, you can read the whole book or dive into chapters where you'd benefit from some learning. A no-nonsense, easy to digest guide for startup and growing businesses alike."

Anj Handa, Founder of Inspiring Women Changemakers

"A very practical hands-on person, I loved the style and language of the book, the quotes along the way and areas to write notes. Jacky knows her stuff when it comes to marketing; excellently written and highly engaging."

Dawn O'Keefe, Co-founder & Managing Director SHINE

How to use this book

From our attitude to money and risk, to brand building and social media. We'll look at the psychological traps we set for ourselves and techniques to help ensure we take good decisions; how to set a price and host an online meeting. We'll take apart a strapline and create an elevator pitch, together with optimising a website and using AI. It's all part and parcel of being in business and it's all important.

Along the way I've added in wisdom from a wide range of people who have, through hard work and self-belief, achieved extraordinary things. They act as signposts for us to follow and reminders that we're all human and that is our strength.

There is space for you to write your own notes and I encourage you to add to each chapter your own ideas, comments and actions.

There are also a range of resources to help you get started.

Contents

The idea for this book grew from my Micro Oiseau project to share free marketing and startup support in different languages. You'll find lots of different birds within the book and, just like us, no matter how the feathers are arranged, I believe we can all succeed and take flight.

www.micro-oiseau.com

Your Mindset

A dive into the mindset for money, wellbeing, engagement and key techniques to support your business.

Begin with Trust

Trust is the invisible X factor in life and in business.

Without it, things never go well.

Think about all the people you trust. And not just the people, how about the trust we put in things created by others for our use: coffee machines, traffic lights, escalators, aeroplanes? It will be a long list.

Now, think about a world devoid of trust; without the many daily actions based on trust in ourselves and others we would probably pull the duvet over our heads and stay in bed.

Who do you trust?

Do you trust yourself?

If you don't trust yourself, why should anybody else trust you?

Before we look at the practical steps and healthy mindset of being in business, getting clear about what trust is, how it works and how important it's going to be to your business is crucial.

In the home and playground, as children we learn the lessons of trust. It is earnt, one action at a time and to do this we learn and employ:

Empathy – understanding and sharing another's point of view.

Kindness – being friendly, considerate and generous.

Reliability – consistently doing what we say we will.

Honesty – being truthful and authentic.

We learn to be cautious and work out who is untrustworthy. We're social creatures, we rely on each other, and trust is key.

Trusting ourselves and trusting others is a strength, not a weakness. It should be the bedrock of your business and part of being trustworthy is being authentic. When we look at how to build a brand, being trustworthy and authentic – our genuine selves, not a version we think we should – or need to be – sits at the heart of all great brands and will be the key to long-term success. Also, not being our true selves is exhausting. It puts up barriers between us and others, which eventually erodes trust, just as honesty and strength of character build it.

Trusting ourselves to do a good job includes resting when we need to; seeking support when we're unsure; checking facts; being courageous; being kind; taking responsibility for our actions and being realistic about our capacity, ability and outcomes.

If you don't trust yourself, how can you expect someone else to trust you?

We need to earn our customers' trust. In turn they'll trust us to deliver what we promise; fix something if it goes wrong; be there for advice; be genuine; be kind and be honest.

Trust is precious. It has built empires. Its loss has also brought them crashing down.

You can't measure it, put it in the bank, borrow or buy it, yet every single successful business on the planet won't survive without it.

When your customers trust you, not only will they be loyal, but they will also tell others about you, and your fledgling business will begin to fly.

"Self-trust is the first secret of success."

Ralph Waldo Emerson
19th century American philosopher, abolitionist and champion of self-reliance.

Ideas and actions...

Risk and Reward
Money: what it really means and what it can do for you?

"Don't make money your goal. Instead, pursue the things you love doing, and then do them so well that people can't take their eyes off you."

Maya Angelou
Multi-award-winning author, composer and civil rights activist.

Your business is not created by money.

Your business is created by your belief, expertise and dedication.

Its success is determined by purpose, execution and profit.

While money may not be the main motivation or goal, making enough to operate as a business and generate profit to help ensure survival and protection, is critical.

In business, as in life, there are two parts to dealing with money successfully:

Our attitude to risk and reward.

The facts to make informed decisions.

The life of your business

Investopedia.com reports that approximately:

33% of businesses fail within the first two years.

50% fail within five years.

Only 33% make it to their tenth year and beyond.

What is also interesting is that these percentages remain the same despite good or bad economic conditions, so there are clearly some key, repeated patterns of human behaviour leading to business failures.

To understand what these behaviours might be, let's look at the top three reasons for business failure:

No market – no need for the goods or services.

No money – cash runs out.

No management – no one knows what they're doing.

If there is no market or need for what you offer, don't waste your time! Research your market BEFORE you spend anything. Be realistic. No matter how much you love the idea and how skilled you may be, is there a need for it? A business that doesn't make a profit is a hobby, and hobbies are great – just not profitable.

Get advice and work out, as far as possible, what money you need to invest and keep the business going until revenue starts to flow in – that includes paying yourself!

Draw up a business plan for the first year. It doesn't need to be complicated but it can help you identify issues before they become a problem.

Good market research, combined with a sound business plan, are both key to good business management.

Get the startup business basics right:

1. Do your research.

2. Seek guidance and support.

3. Understand that customer trust, like profit, needs to be earned.

No one knows all the answers. To survive and thrive in business we all must **learn to run our businesses** by involving mentors and professional experts, and by continually educating ourselves about our market, our customers and the opportunities around us.

As a startup or micro entrepreneur, we may be the only person in the business. We must do everything and this may be why such a high percentage fail within two years. It's hard and often lonely work. Surrounding ourselves with key people that support and guide us will go a long way to keeping us on track.

From the person who does everything, we may join another to form a partnership or become the one that coordinates others to do the work for us by employing staff. At every stage we will make mistakes. That's life. But we stand a much greater chance of succeeding by following and repeating the startup business basics each step of the way.

Our attitude to risk and reward

Our perception of money – what it stands for and what it can do – dominates our lives. It's understandable because money is the medium by which societies around the world operate. For many of us, money is also the measure of 'success'. But success doesn't mean the same for everyone, nor does the amount of money required to feel successful.

Our understanding of what money means to us has a big impact on the way we run our businesses and lives.

Ask yourself:

- Is money a tool to be used, or something to be hoarded and hidden away?

- Is money something I have always had, or never had enough of?

- Does money worry, bore or excite me?

- Do I feel money is something I deserve?

A spreadsheet can record the figures, accounts can outline how a business has managed its affairs throughout the year, yet the answers about how to create and grow a good business will never be found on a spreadsheet.

How we manage our finances is based on what's going on in our heads and our approach to risk and reward.

How many of us allow fear of the unknown to hold back our ambition or blunt our natural talent? The fear of putting faith in our own expertise and experience to realise our dreams? On the other hand, perhaps we know we are impulsive, impatient and bored by detail.

Knowing ourselves, our habits and limits, is just as important as being able to add up and take away, if not more so; understanding how we approach money and, therefore, our strengths and weaknesses, means we're better prepared to run a business.

Ultimately, money is simply a means to an end, and for this reason it's important to know:

WHY we want to start our own business,

WHO is important to it, and

HOW we are going to do it better than anyone else.

It is also helpful to explore our relationship with money because, aside from expertise in our chosen field (unless you are an accountant), very few of us are expert in finance and tax, both of which are important to startup success.

If you feel unsure about managing money, then get advice and professional support.

If you feel confident, still seek advice.

Talk to a local small business accountant or adviser. Seek out a mentor: someone who has been in your position and has made a success of their business. Local business groups often offer support to new startups. Importantly, check your region for local government support schemes and information on the appropriate tax status requirements. Industry organisations also offer a wide range of regulation and finance guidance. Social media can also be helpful in finding groups of sector specific, like-minded businesses that swap knowledge and support.

What we learn will help us avoid making basic mistakes and sidestep problems that could end could end our business before it's even got off the ground.

"Empty pockets never held anyone back. Only empty heads and empty hearts can do that."

Dr Norman Peale
Author of the worldwide best-seller, The Power of Positive Thinking.

Ideas and actions...

The Happy Entrepreneur
How to find the mental freedom to innovate and succeed as a startup

"A bird in a cage is safe but God didn't create birds, for that."

Paulo Coelho
Brazilian novelist and poet.

Many people dream of leaving their nine-to-five job to create their own business, be their own boss and earn an enviable income. So, if all of us are given the same tools – a brain, a body, an idea – why aren't we all successful? Why can't we all be happy entrepreneurs? We're going to look at what it means to take risks, how that impacts our mental health and how we can find the right balance and the resilience to run a successful business.

An entrepreneur is anyone who begins a business or enterprise with the hope of making a profit. Ask any entrepreneur and they will tell you that after the first excitement of launching their own enterprise, they endure a near constant mental battle with "fear and fulfilment": the fulfilment and satisfaction of choosing how they earn their living and the fear of losing it.

So, how do we stay positive, excited by what we're doing and – yes – stay happy?

What do we mean by happy?

Happiness for you is not going to look and feel the same as it does for me. What we need and want in life varies depending on our circumstances and our ambition, yet we all have one thing in common that directly affects our ability to find personal fulfilment, and that's our minds. Our ability to be happy is largely based on how we manage our minds.

Positivity, negativity and fear – we all experience these emotions and we do so for good reason. Over and above an entrepreneur's 'can do' attitude, we need to find the right approach, appreciation and balance of these complex feelings in order to make good decisions and feel good about ourselves.

Good balance in our lives will mean we can enjoy the fun times, be resilient during the hard times and have the mental tools to cope with everything in between. So how do we find this balance?

"Doubt kills more dreams than failure ever will."

Suzy Kassem
American poet and artist.

Fear and fulfilment

Our brain's limbic system directs our bodies to respond instantaneously to intense emotions like anger and fear triggering a fight, flight or freeze response. Because of this ancient 'hard-wired' response mechanism, we unconsciously react in milliseconds before we can consciously process what's happening in front of us. For example, if you don't like spiders or heights you will be very familiar with your limbic system. Along with our species' hard-wiring to avoid hurt, our brains also draw on thousands of our own memories: our unique experiences of fear, shame, confusion, excitement, pain, joy and suspicion.

The problem, however, with our brain's hair-trigger response to a perceived 'threat', is that our minds overreact and can prevent us from achieving what we want.

Self-sabotage

If we've always been told that we won't amount to anything, when faced with a challenge our brains will seek to protect us from embarrassment and failure by placing a big fat doubt in our minds about our ability, even if we have amassed plenty of evidence that proves otherwise. It's self-sabotage. If, on the other hand, we have always been encouraged to try our best and not be afraid, we will have less anxiety about tackling something new. This is, of course, a very simplified example of an extremely complex area, but one thing is true for us all...

Fulfilling our potential means letting go of fear and finding mental freedom

Letting go of fear doesn't mean we should remove fear all together. Just like an early warning system, fear is natural, and for our own safety, we should NOT be completely fearless. If we were, we would walk into the road without checking for traffic, fly a plane without taking a lesson, or agree deadlines that we won't make... It wouldn't go well.

What we can try to do is address our fears to reduce their impact and, by doing so, fulfil our potential and enjoy greater mental freedom.

Some people find it easier than others to control their fear, but no one is immune from nagging doubts; the voice that says: "you can't," "you shouldn't" and of course, "who do you think you are?" It is surprising to discover how many highly experienced professionals suffer from 'imposter syndrome': the feeling they are not good enough, combined with the fear of being 'found out' by others and exposed as a fraud.

In the early '90s I worked in the film industry on a big box office film. Our costume designer was a good person, experienced and talented but continually wracked by self-doubt, which, at times, made them behave badly. This was perhaps more astonishing because the previous year they had won an Oscar. But it didn't matter. Their negative thoughts about themselves, their fear, outweighed the evidence and global appreciation of their many abilities. They couldn't always enjoy their work. They were frequently unhappy and isolated, as they pushed people away.

Fear can be the root of our reactions to different situations and types of people. As well making us anxious, fear can make us jealous, angry, selfish, distant and judgemental. The fear of rejection, just like fear of being found out, can be difficult to overcome.

"The web of our life is of a mingled yarn, good and ill together."

William Shakespeare

At any stage in our lives, fear can trip us up

Separating out natural and useful fears for our safety and 'learned' fears can be the work of years! Learned fears are those we have from childhood, our school years, upbringing and inherited from those with most influence on us. They also come from cultural sources. Women around the world experience fear and often shame from oppressive cultural systems. Boys and men too have different issues around masculinity and expectation. How many of us feel like we have been stripped of our individuality through our education and cultural systems? Our unique qualities are part of our humanity and are the driver of innovation. Being ourselves is essential to the quality of our lives and, ultimately, our ability to succeed as an entrepreneur.

We are all prey to learned fear, but must it control us?

Renowned British psychologist Pippa Grange has written extensively on the subject of fear and invites us to ask ourselves an interesting question:

"Am I performing in life or actually living it?"

When we 'perform' it is unnatural and exhausting. If, on the other hand, we can be our authentic selves, life becomes energising, helping to unleash our potential. As humans we have a fantastic ability for love, fulfilment and joy – there's plenty for everyone. There is no finite amount that is our 'due'.

Pippa also believes that much of our fear is driven by the terms we use. Let's look at 'winning' and 'losing'.

So many things today are judged as either a 'win' or a 'loss' and this simplified 'good' and 'bad' label is as harmful as it is inaccurate. This type of thinking is fear-driven and approaching a situation in a different way can help us move towards our goals with more confidence and less anxiety.

A 'win' is not about your worth as a human being, it is an outcome.

A 'loss' is not about your worth as a human being, it is an outcome.

Thinking of things in this way helps us avoid becoming too inflated with pride AND not too upset when things don't go our way. It also means we can move on faster.

Our worth is what's important. It describes our humanity, our relationships and our unique abilities.

Stuff going our way or not – they are just outcomes.

How we react to winning and losing can make a key difference in achieving a balanced approach to our learning. If we are in control of little else, we are in control of how we choose to react. Think how much more content our lives would be if failure was seen as a learning tool, as opposed to something so often seen as shameful?

"If you're not prepared to be wrong, you'll never come up with anything original."

Ken Robinson
British writer and international adviser on education.

First Attempt In Learning

Many, many highly successful people have cited some of their biggest 'failures' as pivotal moments of change for the better because they learned from them and moved on. Innovation doesn't happen by getting it right, it happens when stuff goes wrong and a new way is found. It can be hard and messy but ...

As your fear diminishes, your confidence grows and gives you more room to get better at what you do. Keep in mind, 'win' or 'lose', our work is our achievement. By focussing on the quality of our work the right outcome will take care of itself.

Sometimes it can also be hard just to begin. When this happens to me, I often say to myself, "What are you waiting for?" because there really is no perfect time to do anything.

If we wait until we are richer, thinner or older; have bought that coat we know we will look great in; the weather is warmer; we've rearranged the house or taken the dog for a walk ... we can convince ourselves never to begin anything. You'll be amazed how much easier it becomes once you take the first step.

"I wonder if fears ever really go away, or if they just lose their power over us."

Veronica Roth
Best-selling American author.

Think about what you want to do, write it down and complete the first task on your list. Take that first step then keep going...

When a negative becomes a positive

US therapist Whitney Goodman talks about 'toxic positivity' in her best-selling book of the same name. Counselling cancer patients early in her career, Goodman realised that unending positivity was creating a harmful disconnect with the wider world. She writes:

"Sometimes things are hard because they're just hard and not because you're incompetent... It's OK to complain about something you're grateful for."

Goodman also puts her finger on something else. The recent wellness 'revolution' has generated an abundance of life coaches being relentlessly upbeat, as if positivity has become "a goal and an obligation" in itself.

Positivity and negativity are two sides of the same coin. We can't have one without the other. Both give our life meaning. To find balance, we need to pay attention to both. Sadly, we've got a bit of challenge here as well!

The phenomenon of humans remembering negative, or upsetting, things more frequently and in greater detail than positive ones is described by psychologists as 'negative bias'. Who hasn't been having a great day for one misplaced comment from a friend or colleague to upset us, outweighing all the good things that had happened? And who doesn't have a crushingly embarrassing teenage moment that we still replay in our minds (when everyone else involved has long forgotten it)? It's crazy, but it's true! Remember, when our brain registers a perceived 'threat' it will bring it to our attention. That threat could be a mean comment, pushing away the other happier and often more important things in our day. It's how we're wired as humans; we can't help it, but we can help ourselves deal with it.

The highs and lows in business can come thick and fast. The excitement of attracting clients, receiving investment and great customer feedback; the anxiety of losing business to a competitor, being criticised by someone, or making a poor judgement call; the drudgery of paperwork and loneliness. Many startups and small businesses begin with just one person and it can be a scary place. No one is immune to fear, it is how we react that makes the difference and why some people are more successful than others.

Evidence is a powerful tool to help us keep balance. Asking ourselves, what is really going on here? Why am I upset? And, importantly, what can I do about it? Collecting evidence, coming to a reasonable conclusion and taking action, no matter how small, can help us be OK with life's ups and downs. It can also give us some perspective on a situation that might otherwise have upset us for days.

Positive or negative, we need to acknowledge ALL our feelings, so that we can get benefit from the wisdom they give us. Regret and sadness can make us better people. In a life well lived there should be both happy and painful experiences. Fewer painful ones of course, but, if we had no negative feelings, how would we recognised and appreciate the good times? How would we make better decisions if we had nothing to learn from? Forget what hurt you in the past, but never forget what it taught you.

Many psychologists now recognise that temporary sadness is a 'problem-solving' emotion – an important function of better decision making, along with research from academics around the world telling us that accepting temporary sadness can improve our attention to detail, increase perseverance, promote generosity and make us more grateful for what we've got. Crying, as an expression of sadness, is also an effective form of self-soothing. That's why we feel so much better after a good cry. I feel it's a shame that men are sometimes seen as weak when they cry. It is natural and it's important. It would also appear that trying to avoid feelings of sadness can make us feel worse.

Regrets are important for our maturity. Daniel Pink, the author of *The Power of Regret* insists, "Banishing them is a bad strategy... Regrets clarify what matters to us and teach us how to do better. That's the power of this emotion – if we treat it right."

Pay attention!

To help ourselves we need to pay attention.

When we feel an uncomfortable emotion, we often ignore it. We may not feel we have time or be in the right place to process why we're feeling angry, anxious or upset. For example, a meeting with clients would not be a good time to stop, mid-sentence, to consider why we feel a sense of dread. Being curious about our emotions, however, and understanding why we feel the way we do, is an important way to gain self-knowledge, perspective and the mental freedom and balance we're looking for.

So where do we start? First, we must acknowledge WHAT we are feeling. Listen to yourself and sit with that emotion. Where is it? Your head, your stomach, your lower back? Recognise it and give it some space by seeing what happens when you give it your attention. What comes to mind as you do so? Breathe.

From personal experience, an anger I often felt in a particular situation tracked back to part of my early childhood and a confusing, lonely and frightening time for me. Gradually, by listening and being curious about my anger, instead of acting on it or dismissing it, I came to realise what was going on and began, with help, to address and let go of my childhood fears. My anger, the manifestation of my fear, also then disappeared.

We can have all the checklists and goals in the world, but without checking in with ourselves regularly they won't amount to much.

When we feel upset, try, in that moment, to hold that feeling and think about what triggered it; what might be sitting underneath your first reaction. What might be driving that fear? By exploring our fears, we can find better balance and greater confidence to follow our goals because we are not carrying the baggage that might sabotaged our efforts.

It is equally important to feel joyful and enjoy good times, spreading that joy to everyone who touches our lives.

Be grateful and get on

Comparison with other people and businesses is as damaging as it is pointless.

Social media is very good at distracting us with other people's 'successes' and 'beautiful lives'. If you recognise that creeping feeling of, "I'll never be as good/as wealthy/as smart/as young/as brave as … remind yourself that:

Social media can be a great tool. It can also be an unhelpful, distorted, airbrushed, bottomless pit.

In reality:

- We all start from different places
- We all have different strengths
- We are all on different journeys
- We are all worthy of success

It's important to focus on what we can do with the resources and time we have RIGHT NOW and stop wasting our time giving others our precious attention.

Let's be grateful for the people, places and things that sustain us. Let's take control and refocus on our own ambition.

There is a large body of evidence that says taking some time every day to identify and be grateful changes our brain chemistry for the better. When we acknowledge, express and receive gratitude, our brains increase our levels of serotonin and dopamine and reduce levels of cortisol. Serotonin and dopamine are neurotransmitters responsible for our emotions and they make us feel good. Cortisol increases when we feel anxious or stressed.

"Gratitude turns what we have into enough."

Aesop
Greek slave and storyteller, 620 BCE.

The impact of regularly practising gratitude can help, not only put us in a good mood, but also support greater resilience and better decision making.

Giving thanks can make us happier and more accepting, and give us the mental freedom to move on.

People Power

Telling others about our feelings, good and bad, also has the effect of lightening the weight and loosening the baggage. There is an old English proverb: "A problem shared is a problem halved." When we discuss what's bothering us with a trusted colleague or friend, language has a way of helping us order our thoughts and move us on towards working out what to do, even if the other person never says a word!

The people we surround ourselves with are critical to our happiness. As well as being supportive and fun to be around, unfortunately some can drain us of energy and confidence, manipulate us and create a negative environment. Their fears and inadequacies are looking for company and, as well as making us miserable, whether they realise it or not, they are damaging to our self-esteem. This type of person can distract and delay us from what we really should be doing, and that's finding and sticking with the supportive people who share our vision and are good to be around.

It is true that we can't choose our family, but we can choose an entrepreneurial 'family' – a network or community who can support our ideas and enterprise, as well as our moments of doubt.

This is especially important for lone entrepreneurs and startups. People to turn to for advice when the going gets tough can make all the difference. Repaying the favour to others in a similar situation helps build trust and opens the door to collaboration. None of us can be an expert in all the different areas needed to run a business and we'll always be better at some things than others. Great innovation often comes from recognising what we're good at, seeking out others with complementary skills and having the confidence to take it for a test drive. My guide Be Successful: how to collaborate looks at this in more detail with some great examples that may surprise you.

When the going gets tough

Something that can often help to de-escalate emotions in a difficult situation, is to be angry at the situation, not the person(s). Removing personal blame means more quickly addressing the actual issue and working out how to solve it, and ensuring it doesn't happen again. Reflection after the issue has been dealt with could mean a system change, a training need or, possibly, addressing a difficult relationship, but that can be done better and more thoughtfully in a calmer, more reflective way after the event, rather than in the heat of the moment.

Putting in boundaries that protect us is also important. By this I mean working out what works best for us to maintain good mental and physical health. Where we work, how long, with whom and how. We can't fully control our environments, but we can make choices about how we respond to situations. Eating lunch away from our desks, switching off our phones after 7pm, taking a 15 minute walk in nature, checking in with friends; these are important choices for self-care. Boundaries, in this sense, are not limitations, they are there to protect and promote our wellbeing.

Finally, don't forget to celebrate the wins. Take time to reflect and feel good about how far you have come and, whatever the win – no matter how small – be proud. Take pride in yourself, your team and all your supporters and customers, remembering that:

Good people are the key to a happy life.

Integrity and authenticity are the key to self-respect.

Trust is the key to good business.

Finding balance in your mental and physical health is a big part of being a happy entrepreneur. Balance will give you the mental strength to take on all the inevitable challenges that being in business will bring. It will enable you to cope with the tough times and mean you can enjoy the good times and the results of all your hard work with the people you love.

"The opposite of fear is mental freedom."

Pippa Grange
British applied psychologist and author.

Be true to yourself.

Know yourself and who's got your back – that's when you'll flourish and find the mental freedom of a happy entrepreneur.

Let's begin...

What you can do **right now** to begin achieving better balance.

1. Give yourself a little space every day. Find a place that is away from movement and noise and just allow yourself some stillness. Just be. Pay attention to what your mind and body is telling you.

2. Take some deep breaths. Don't expect anything. Don't reject anything.

3. Think about something you thought of as a 'loss'. Now, think of it as just an outcome:

   - What did it teach you?

   - What decision will you make differently now?

   - Write it down, so that you can remember what happened and how you dealt with it.

4. Be grateful for what you have and appreciate others.

5. Identify someone you can trust and make a time to talk. Make a date in your diary.

6. Think about what feeds your 'energy': family, friends, hobbies, nature? Ensure you do it regularly. If it helps put a reminder in your diary.

Who and what can help

Networking face-to-face or online groups are a good source of support. Explore a few and find a like-minded community to share with. Not only will you find support but also the potential for partnership and collaboration through shared aims and ambition.

Business mentors are usually already successful in a particular field and can be of great help talking things over and assessing situations. With no specific agenda, mentoring relationships can last years, offering plenty of guidance and support. It never hurts to ask!

A business coach, just like an athletics coach, helps people achieve a particular professional goal or address an issue, with an agreed timespan and outcome in mind.

Pressure is important, stress is destructive. Read our free guide *A Short Guide to Stress and How to Deal with It* by forensic psychologist and resilience expert Dr Jo Clarke PhD https://micro-oiseau.com/more-help-for-entrepreneurs/stress-and-how-to-deal-with-it

Supportive resources, music, self-care, exercise, culture – know what gives you peace and practise regularly.

If you struggle with emotions or behaviours that repeatedly impact negatively on your life, it's important to give yourself the opportunity to heal and fulfil your potential. A psychiatrist or psychotherapist is a good way to address personal issues, all of which will affect your professional life.

"You can't make decisions based on fear and the possibility of what might happen."

Michelle Obama
Lawyer and author, First Lady of United States, 2009 – 2017.

Ideas and actions...

How to Collaborate

Collaboration is two or more people working together towards a shared goal. When we collaborate, we create, we improve and we solve problems, and, more often than not, we do it faster and better than we would do alone.

In this chapter we explore examples of great collaboration, the lessons we can learn and count down the top ten tips of how to collaborate successfully.

"None of us is as smart as all of us."

Kenneth Blanchard
Business Consultant and author of The One Minute Manager *selling over 15 million copies worldwide.*

Before we begin... It's worth noting that collaboration is NOT the same as cooperation.

Collaboration means two or more people supporting each other to achieve the same goal.

Cooperation, on the other hand, means two or more people supporting each other to achieve their own separate goals.

A good example of collaboration would be a band: a group of people playing different instruments to produce the same tune. They all have different skills but the goal is single, shared and harmonious.

Collaboration is the secret AND the key to many a successful business and world-changing innovation.

Collaboration is a way of thinking

Let's explore collaboration. Find out about the benefits it brings and how you can collaborate to increase your chances of success!

Sometimes collaboration can feel effortless. Sometimes it can be frustrating. Sometimes disappointing, but without collaboration we wouldn't have the lifestyle, culture and technology we enjoy today.

Without collaboration countless great ideas and inventions wouldn't have got off the ground.

Humans are hard-wired to collaborate

Collaboration requires people to share what they know to create something bigger and better than they could achieve on their own.

Over many thousands of years humans have been hard-wired to share skills for survival; to hunt for larger prey and build stronger shelters to better protect family groups.

Today, although we may not need to fend off a sabre-tooth tiger or build our own homes, we are no different in that we all have skills we can combine with others to achieve a common purpose. When we do this we become stronger, wiser and more resilient.

In order to collaborate well we need to be open to new ideas, new opportunities and ways of doing things. We need to be able to SHARE.

"Following a plan is good for progress. Opportunity, however, usually exists off the plan."

Simon Sinek

British-born author of Start with Why - *how great leaders inspire everyone to take action.*

Be open to opportunity

Being open-minded and curious about everything and everyone will mean that you are far more likely to spot a great opportunity. It is also often true that these opportunities come from unexpected places, including this great example of successful collaboration between medicine and fashion.

Dr Roger Kneebone (as his name suggests!) is a doctor and professor at Imperial College in London. Dr Kneebone also has a reputation for unusual and creative collaborations to solve problems. One of these collaborations has been his work with the famous English tailor Patrick Grant.

Dr Kneebone was concerned about patients who were struggling with recovering from their surgical wounds. These wounds could be slow and painful to heal. In particular, Dr Kneebone noticed that a lot of problems were caused by the poor stitching of the surgeons. It was clear that surgeons were so focussed on the medical procedure that their ability to sew neatly, or at all, was not questioned.

Dr Kneebone turned to expert tailor Patrick Grant, who agreed to collaborate with a group of surgeons on developing new stitching techniques. The collaboration of tailor and surgeon resulted in faster, neater and better stitching with patients recovering quicker, needing less pain medication and with fewer scars.

If you had the choice between a surgeon who understood the benefits of neat stitching and could sew, and one who just gave it their best shot, which one would you choose?

Often you need to look outside your experience and expertise to improve something or solve a problem. Creative collaboration means watching out for and welcoming new and sometimes surprising collaborators.

Find out more about Professor Roger Kneebone and his enlightening collaborations.

A collaborative mind is curious and democratic.

Ask yourself, "How can my skills be used to solve a problem?"

Good collaboration leads to improvement

Great collaboration leads to innovation

"I'm going to put a thousand songs in your pocket."

Steve Jobs
American Inventor of the iPod. Former CEO of Apple.

New products like the first iPod, or new business structures like Uber, don't just improve the way we do things, they change them forever.

Today, the sheer complexity and increasing number of questions needing answers is forcing us to collaborate, especially in science where projects require more knowledge than any one individual can possess.

Our first example of a highly successful collaboration is the twelve founding member states and scientists that established CERN (Conseil Européen pour la Recherche Nucléaire) one of the longest and most successful collaborations in the history of science.

Sharing ideas, knowledge and costs for decades, today Europe still dominates the field of particle physics. And that's not all CERN has been responsible for... How about the World Wide Web?

In 1989 while working at CERN, British computer scientist Tim Berners-Lee came up with the idea to help him communicate and collaborate more efficiently with colleagues. Fast forward to today and the Internet underpins much of our home and work lives around the globe.

We are also using past and present collaboration to help inform our future.

A 'Hive Mind' describes mass collaboration of many people working together to solve or address an issue.

Every day for the past 200 years, sea captains all around the globe recorded the weather and sea temperature in their logs. This vast, untapped knowledge is now the focus of a massive collaborative effort by scientists supported by the general public. Volunteers transcribing ships' logs in order to collate weather and sea temperature data into one vast database. Scientists will then use the database to help today's oceanographers map and measure changes in sea temperatures as our climate warms.

Top ten tips on how to collaborate well

Here's our check list to ensure that everyone wins!

1. **Is collaboration what you need?**
    Collaboration is NOT a way of getting what you want cheaper and more easily. So, think about your goal. Could it be achieved in another way? For example, by taking a course, getting a loan, recruiting more staff or sub-contracting work?

2. **Assess your risk versus reward**
    Collaboration brings risk. Take your time to review any proposed collaboration and work out the risks and rewards for you and your business. What might you gain and what might you lose? Importantly, what are you prepared to lose? Is the time and effort worth the rewards you seek? Do you walk away or take a 'leap of faith'?

3. **Find the right partners**
    The right collaborators don't need to be like you, but they must respect your skills and way of working. Many collaborations don't get off the ground because of mismatched expectations, goals, skills and resources. There is no point collaborating with anyone who doesn't bring additional skills and resources to complement yours, or, who simply wants to take advantage of you. (See point 1)

Who do you already know?

The best collaborations are often with people you already know,even if the project needs new ways of thinking. If you need different resources or skills your colleagues and current connections may be, or know, the right people.

Larry Page met Sergey Brin at Stanford University. Larry offered to give Sergey a tour of the campus. The two young men discovered that they had a common interest in Internet search algorithms. They liked each other and stayed in touch. Some years later Larry and Sergey got together and went on to start a company that would become Google.

Nuture your small ideas and early friendships: who knows where they can take you.

5. **Find common ground**
    Need, opportunity and collaboration can create the beautiful, the diverse and the delicious!

    Ben Cohen and Jerry Greenfield were childhood best friends and, after leaving college, wanted to set up in business together. They decided to open a bagel shop. Sadly, the equipment was too expensive, so, instead they opted for making ice cream. They took a $5 correspondence course in ice cream making and in 1978 rented an old renovated petrol station. Shortly after, Ben and

Jerry's Homemade Ice Cream opened for business and, because Ben didn't have a good sense of smell or taste, they focussed on intense flavours and big chunky bits. It was a personal preference that would be a hit with ice cream lovers all around the world!

Stay true to your goals and the way you like to do things. There are others out there that will agree.

6. **Build relationships, trust and ground rules**
Collaborations don't happen between algorithms, websites or organisations, they happen between people, and they succeed through trust and a common bond. When you have identified who you'd like to collaborate with, establish the ground rules and ensure you fully understand everyone's skills and responsibilities. How will problems be handled? Who will contribute what? How will rewards be split?

Gabrielle Bonheur "Coco" Chanel was a French fashion designer and founder of the Chanel brand. She is also the only fashion designer listed on Time magazine's list of the 100 most influential people of the 20th century. Incredibly, Coco only owned 10% of her business. The other 90% was controlled by her financier Pierre Wertheimer. Coco had ambition but she didn't have money. Wertheimer recognised Coco's amazing potential but he wasn't artistic. By partnering with Wertheimer, Coco kept complete creative control over her brand and had access to financial expertise, business connections and funding. Ultimately, both Coco and Pierre became very wealthy by recognising and respecting the skills of the other and collaborating on their common goal to achieve global success.

Egos have no place in collaboration. Respect does. Decide what your goals are. They won't always be money.

7. **Eliminate the toxic**
    It happens. There may be one or two people in any collaboration that don't put in the same effort as everyone else. This may be because they don't have the right skills, they are too busy, their circumstances change, or maybe they are just too lazy! Whatever it is, it can break trust and ruin a project. After talking over the issue, give them a second chance if they ask for it. If the situation continues, it is time to go your separate ways. It's important not to ignore or reward poor performance, you will regret it.

8. **Find your champions and sponsors**
    Everyone needs supporters. A 'champion' knows your goals and is good at building relationships with a good network of their own. They can help keep the project focussed and keep up momentum. They are great to have around. Sponsors are great for endorsing and showcasing your work to attract funding, interest and resources. Make sure they know all your good news stories so that they can spread the word. Your sponsors may also be able to bring on board more collaborators if you need them.

9. **Care for your collaboration**
    Collaboration can be hard work. Pace yourself and bring in new people when you need to. If you do, make sure they know your shared values and goals to help keep the positive energy going and build on your efforts. Regularly check in with how your collaborators are feeling and tap into their energy when you need to. Let them do the same in return. We all have days when we need a hand up.

10. **Measure, monitor and talk about your success**
    Small wins, big wins, they are all important to keeping a collaboration on track, so celebrate and talk about

them. The leaps of understanding and moments of clarity, the milestones and the breakthroughs. Use your Champions and Sponsors, social media and personal networks to talk about your progress. Measure and monitor the results to lean how to better focus your communication.

Finally, we can learn from great examples of collaboration in the natural world.

Shared purpose isn't just for humans

Social weaver birds are a collaborative inspiration. Found in southern Africa, these tiny birds achieve group strength and protection in numbers through the collaborative building of huge communal nests. Similar to our apartment blocks, the nests have many levels and different sized 'rooms', protecting the birds from predators, as well as the scorching sun and freezing night temperatures. Regularly maintained by the birds, the nests offer safe and happy homes to generations.

True collaboration means that everyone wins

In the lean winter months wolves and ravens collaborate to ensure everyone gets fed. Circling high over the land, ravens can more easily spot the wolf's prey. Once spotted they land nearby and croak noisily. The birds are, in fact, guiding the wolves to their next meal. In return the wolves appear happy for the ravens to feast on the carcasses they leave behind and are tolerant of their presence at kills.

Different skills mean different approaches with one goal – survival

The formidable Colombian lesserblack tarantula could easily eat an animal as small as the dotted humming frog, but it doesn't. In fact, the giant spider and tiny frog are happy to share the same home. This strange domestic arrangement has developed because the predators that eat dotted humming frogs don't dare enter the burrow of a large hunting spider. Protected from attack by the presence of the spider, the tiny frog feasts on the beetles and ants that are attracted to the spider's kills, including those that eat the spider's eggs. So, contrary to an earlier theory that the frog was the spider's pet, the frog is, in fact, protecting the next generation of Colombian lesserblacks which, in turn, provide safe homes for the next generation of dotted humming frogs.

Never underestimate your worth or think you are too small to make an impact.

"Never doubt that a small group of thoughtful, committed citizens can change the world. Indeed, it is the only thing that ever has."

Margaret Mead
American cultural anthropologist.

How to Make Good Choices

After taking the decision to begin a business, we are faced with a lot of choices, which will mean gathering information, weighing up options and coming to conclusions on a whole range of things. Good early choices will form the bedrock of your long-term success.

Some people appear to be able to make decisions quickly and confidently. Others less so, and, apart from the required expertise or knowledge, the reason for many decisions being difficult lies in the very nature of what a decision is: a commitment to act.

The reality about how and what we choose to do, lies in a complex response to our environment, shaped by our unique experiences, education, influences and personality. Our approach also depends on the type of decision we have before us: from which toothpaste to buy to which domain name, business partner, bank loan or life partner.

To help us make good decisions we're going to look at:

1. Rational and irrational styles of decision making

2. Advice from Ancient Rome

3. The Devil's Advocate

4. Self-knowledge

5. The benchmark for better

1. Rational and irrational decision making

A rational style means choices made by gathering information to arrive at a range of alternatives which, based on benefits, costs and potential impact, leads to a conclusion about a course of action.

An irrational style means choices made based on personal values and beliefs, an emotional response that can bring personal satisfaction and fulfilment.

Both styles are important and useful, depending on our needs, circumstances and values. For example, choosing the right bank account from a range of options means that a strategic, evidence-driven approach will help us make the best choice whereas, choosing a charity to support means we draw on our personal beliefs to satisfy our values.

The key is to recognise which approach is best for which situation because when we get it wrong, we're likely to make poor decisions with equally poor, if not potentially disastrous, results...

We choose a business savings account because the sun is out, the brochure is in our favourite colour and the advert includes a cat (just like our much-loved family pet). Our irrational decision means we've put a lot of money into an account that we can't access when we need it, for a small gain in interest.

A better choice would have been a rational approach to research the different savings options, get advice from a financial expert and think about our future business needs.

We choose a well-known, well-run international charity to support because it has a high profile; there are many news articles discussing its work with many brand and celebrity endorsements. Yet, our rational decision here clashes with our personal values of supporting our local community. It means our commitment and subsequent donations are low, we feel personally dissatisfied and disassociated, quickly losing interest.

A better choice would have been more irrational, choosing a local small cat sanctuary where we could offer more tangible support, giving us far greater personal fulfilment, interest and creating long-term commitment. Ultimately, a far better result for the charity and us.

2. Advice from Ancient Rome - Illeism

When our friends come to us for advice, we can often be calm and wise, gathering evidence and information, giving different alternatives and generally being supportive and helping them find a solution. Yet, we can struggle to apply this wisdom to our own decision making. We may be great at helping others make choices at work or in their personal life, but we're hopeless when faced with the same situation ourselves. What's happening? Our emotions are clouding our judgement, previous mistakes making us overly critical and defensive. Ultimately, we make poor choices for ourselves.

From the Latin word "ille" meaning "he" or "that", Illeism describes how we can talk about ourselves in the third person instead of the first person. For example, using 'they' instead of 'I'. It was a technique used by the Roman Emperor Julius Caesar in his speeches, and you'll hear Illeisum used in politics and literature.

Award-winning science writer David Robson proposes that we can use this technique to help make better decisions for ourselves. Psychologists have found that using Illeism alters the way we think and we can make use of this 'mind trick' to help our decision making. We simply talk about our situation and the decision before us in the third person, and approach it as if we are advising a friend. For example, I would say:

"Jacky can't decide whether to buy a laptop or a desktop computer for her business."

I would carry on discussing my thoughts around the subject:

"She is worried about space in her home, as she doesn't have an office yet, and wonders if a laptop would be a good short-term investment, or should she…"

The technique works because it moves us out of our emotional state and gives us psychological distance from our feelings. Scientific experiments using Illeism found that people got a better, broader perspective, allowing them to see the bigger picture; they became less self-critical and more open to new possibilities. And, the more people practised, the better they got at balanced reasoning, which improved their general decision making over time.

Why not try Illeism for your next decision and see if this ancient technique can give you greater clarity? Keep going and see how it helps you!

3. The Devil's Advocate

When we begin in business, we are most likely to start out on our own or with one other person. Having another person with whom to discuss options is good but can lead to deadlock if we hold an opposing view to our business partner. Whichever your situation, there is a great way to make difficult decisions that offers confidence and clarity in our choices.

This type of decision making is done by a group. Sole entrepreneurs often use trusted associates or experienced colleagues, mentors and friends to help them, and the same is true for business partners. Here's how it works:

- One person will lead the group discussion around the case for making a specific decision.

- One person in the group will play Devil's Advocate and their role is to argue against the proposed decision.

- A third person will act as an impartial observer. Their

role is to listen to the discussion and play back to the group how they came to the decision.

A great way to get clarity about a difficult choice, this format helps unmask bias and expose unreliable information and expose unreliable information and weak logic, and ensure that the decision reached is the best, most reasoned choice for the business.

4. A little self-knowledge goes a long way – MoralDNA®

Roger Steare thinks a lot about how people think and make decisions.

Given our different education, upbringing, culture, environment and location, is there a way for us all to make good choices and do the right thing, thus creating a more content, positive and better world? The result of Roger's busy mind is the MoralDNA® project.

MoralDNA® is a worldwide research initiative led by Roger, in partnership with Pavlos Stampoulidis, Director of Psycholate. It is a free online questionnaire with the aim of helping people understand what influences them and what is important to them, regardless of their age, location or occupation.

When you respond to the short MoralDNA® questionnaire, you will be asked a series of questions about yourself and your decision making preferences. Only taking around five minutes to complete, it is completely free and, upon completion, you will receive a personalised analysis that reveals your decision making preferences and ethical behaviour. It can even give you an understanding of how your behaviour differs at home and at work.

"Doing the right thing isn't always easy, yet, understanding how we make up our minds means we're more likely to do the right thing, in the right way more, of the time."

Roger Steare

Visit the MoralDNA® project today and find out if you are an Angel, a Teacher or a Governor – or maybe a Guardian, a Judge or a Philosopher – and discover what this means for your decision making.

Roger also offers a free eBook *How to Do What's Right*.

5. The basics for better decision making

- Source accurate information. Rarely, if ever, has a good decision been made based on hearsay, rumour or 'fake' information drawn from unverified sources. This also applies to opinions of well-meaning friends and family members; they may believe they have our best interests at heart, but do they know what they are talking about? Their point of view will be affected by their own fears, biases and experiences.

- Talk to people with the right knowledge and experience. Getting tax advice from anyone other than an accountant, or medical advice from anyone other than a doctor, is as pointless as it is potentially disastrous.

- Read trusted news sources, a mix of recognised national and regional platforms that offer impartial reporting of facts.

- Listen to scientists. Real ones, doing funded research

in verified institutions. Science matters. It is how we save lives and how we know we are in a climate crisis.

· Watch out for personal bias. Reject stereotypes. Judge people on personal interactions, support talent, commitment and enthusiasm.

· Talk to trusted friends and mentors. Being vulnerable and seeking advice may feel difficult, yet it's often one of the best things we can do to find clarity.

· Listen to your instincts. Our unique life experience means we have sub-conscious reactions to situations. I call them my 'alarm bells', for others it is their 'gut instinct', 'sixth sense' or 'intuition'; picking up on valuable social cues, it's important to take notice. Mine are rarely, if ever, wrong.

· Learn from your mistakes because next time you'll make a better decision.

· Know nothing stays the same. Tastes, markets, technology, materials and people change. We can only go on the information we have at the time and should never be afraid to change our minds and review a decision, adjust an approach and make better decisions accordingly.

Finally...

Once you have made a decision around a goal, take action.

In the moment you decide on a course of action, do something that will help you achieve it, or else it is unlikely to happen.

Writing it down is a start. Make a date in a diary; begin a conversation, a check list or a change in routine; book an event, a course or appointment.

"The secret to getting things done is to act."

Dante Aligheri
Fouteenth century Italian poet, philosopher, writer and one of the Western world's greatest literary icons.

Ideas and actions...

Celebrate the wins, however small. It's not about coming first, it's about your firsts.

The Coin Flip Trick

My daughter is autistic. She is bright and high functioning but can often find making decisions particularly difficult.

Having thought about the options and potentially different outcomes to a decision, if she still just can't decide she uses a psychological trick to find out what she REALLY wants to do.

She will toss a coin, attributing one side to choice A and the other side choice B. Whichever side lands facing up, that's the choice to take.

She explains:

"When the coin lands, I gauge my reaction. If I'm relieved with the outcome then I'm happy, that's the right choice and the decision is made.

"If I find I am immediately disappointed with the outcome, I know that the other option was the one I really wanted all along. It always works for me!"

If you find yourself disappointed or uncomfortable with a decision you've made.

Stop and think again.

Revisit the facts and the potential outcomes. Try to pinpoint why you aren't comfortable. Talk it over with someone who will be unaffected by the outcome.

How many times do we say to ourselves, "I knew I shouldn't have done that!" when the damage is done?

"Success isn't about the end result, it's about what you learn on the way."

Vera Wang

American fashion designer who initially pursued a career in figure skating, competing at the 1968 US Figure Skating Championships.

Ideas and actions...

Meaningful engagement is built, not bought.

What and Why People Share
and how that helps you

Social media is a way of talking about what you do to people who are looking for what you sell.

Designed to democratise communication and global conversations, social media can be informative, influencing and fun, enabling us to find and keep in touch with family, friends, colleagues, suppliers, associates and a bunch of new like-minded people we can learn from. Think of platforms including X, Facebook, Instagram, TikTok, LinkedIn, YouTube, Pinterest, Vimeo, Tumblr, Reddit, Weixin/WeChat, WhatsApp, Snapchat ... the list goes on and on, with the top platforms being used by billions of us around the world.

59% of the world uses social media every day

As of January 2023, research by GWI, formerly GlobalWebIndex, tells us that 59% of the world's population use social media for an average of two and a half hours a day. That's over 4.7 billion people browsing, scrolling, messaging and clicking, and this continues to rise.

Less appealingly, social media is also used by some to amplify prejudice, encourage misinformation and prey on the vulnerable, through algorithms that put profit before people. Addictive by design, social media presents us with a marketing opportunity but, because of these issues, for any business or organisation, the decision to use social media is both a personal and a business one: both emotional and strategic.

Quality v Quicksand

As a startup, it's likely that we'll be the one making all the decisions; perhaps there is another or a small group of key individuals. The values, or business ethos, we hold should run like veins through our brand thinking and will inform how we choose to communicate with the world, as well as how we package our goods and sell our services.

The positives of social media marketing outweigh the negatives for startups and business, but only if:

- Engagement is aligned with the values of the brand (emotional).

- Delivery of content is underpinned by a knowledgeable and planned approach (strategic). This strategy should include ensuring that whatever your social media is directing people towards, it will be worth their time. A website, blog page, newsletter – whatever it is, it needs to be well designed, fully functioning, easy to use and search engine optimised.

This emotional and strategic approach will help ensure we are living our values and managing our time and input in the most efficient way to benefit our business.

The question now is, how do we build awareness and market our businesses via social media? The answer lies in what the people we want to attract like to read and, just as importantly, what they like to share.

What do people share?

Social media platforms differ in prominence of content, be that text, image or video. Dependent on your customers' preferences, whichever you choose it's wise to have quality in everything you present.

Why do people share?

No matter the language or culture, there are some things that we all have in common. We all like stories, new ideas, tips and free stuff, whether that be the latest news, a clever way to do something, a warning of potential danger or something funny. We like knowing these things and we also like to share them because it raises our status with others.

If you think about the audience we want to engage for our business through social media, we have an idea of our customer – their likes and dislikes – and, as such, which platform they are most likely to inhabit (it could well be more than one). The strategy behind our social media marketing is to create content that makes the audience feel valued with the potential to raise their status within networks that are likely to have similar likes and dislikes.

Do you want to feel special, intelligent and loved?

I do.

When someone makes me feel special, intelligent and loved I love them right back. Well, I certainly like them and feel a sense of loyalty to them. Supplying content that hits all these buttons through your social media channel (indeed all your customer engagements) is going to help you establish and build an audience of followers that is quite happy and prepared to engage with you and share your content to their networks.

Followers feel special when they are offered an 'exclusive': a discount or access to helpful resources; the ability to ask direct questions and get helpful information back.

Followers feel intelligent when they get good free advice and in sharing it, they in turn become a recognised source of valuable information.

Followers feel loved when they feel we are thinking of them: we care about their issues and are working to make their lives easier.

Facts and feelings

I am writing about how we can make people feel. That's because feelings, our emotions, are at the centre of our decision making process. We can't help it. No decision we EVER make is completely objective because from the moment we can make up our own minds we do so based on our past and current experiences of trust, betrayal, love, frustration, fear, greed, loyalty, contentment, education and the emotional traces they leave with us.

The science behind this lies deep within our brains in a cluster of neurons called the amygdala. Part of the limbic system, neuroscientists believe that our amygdala governs our emotions, as well as having a role in our decision making. If you want someone to make a decision, as well as presenting the facts, you'll need to take into account the way they are feeling in that moment too.

So as well as the facts, how people feel about your content will make them like it, share it, act on it or bin it.

To help work out the kind of content to create, think about the following elements:

value – informative, useful

currency – newsworthy, trending

story – inspiration, journey, vision

emotion – desire, joy, relief, envy, fear, humour

Think about the kind of content you receive and like to share – not necessarily on social media – and you'll find that you, along with everyone else around the world, responds to the same things.

Within our social media strategies – from how many times we post content, to when and what we post – we should try to use an engaging mix of value, currency, story and emotion, all making people feel special, intelligent and loved. Picking content that touches on these elements hooks in to our human needs and desires and THAT'S what we like and share. It will make your social media strategy grow the awareness and reach you're looking for.

Make sure you read our marketing guide *Be heard: how to get results from social media* for more on creating successful social media campaigns.

Online communities

Whatever you're interested in, there's likely to be an online forum or community that is very happily discussing, comparing and dissecting the topic. When researching your market and exploring social media platforms, online communities can be a valuable source of information. Reddit, for example, is one of the largest online community platforms worldwide with over 100,000 active 'subreddits' or communities, used by millions daily.

A good way to get involved with your audience and potential customers, find collaborators and unearth competitors, online communities offer a space to listen, learn and share. The best community platforms combine friendly forums, private messaging, live chat, discussion boards and video. If you decide to create your own online community in support of your business, you'll find a wide choice of platforms to choose from and plenty of advice available to help you begin. Starting with a free to create Facebook group, other popular platforms include Discord, Tribe, Circle, Discourse and Slack.

"Passion is energy. Feel the power that comes from focusing on what excites you."

Oprah Winfrey

American talk show host, producer, actress, author, and media proprietor.

Ideas and actions...

Your Marketing

Our Micro Oiseau Marketing Guides, brought together in one easy-to-read section for dipping in and out of, as and when you need them.

Be Noticed: how to build a great brand

Be Valued: how to set the right price and sell

Be Seen: how to develop your marketing plan

Be Seen Online: how to develop a good website

Be Persuasive: how to advertise

Be Heard: how to get results from social media

Be Professional: how to make a great first impression

Be Professional Online: how to prepare for virtual meetings

If you've got this far and you are thinking

Is it the right time?

There's no 'right' time. There is just now.

So, let's begin...

Be Noticed: how to build a great brand

As individuals we all have our own personal 'brand' – our personality, if you like – made up of:

How we appear and what we wear.

How we talk and what we say.

How we treat ourselves, other people and the things around us.

Our image, communication and behaviour affect our ability to influence others and it is the same for a business. It does not matter if that business has one, 10, or 10,000 employees, a brand is not simply a logo, a brand is everything about that business. Brand matters because it persuades people to buy.

It's also a comforting thought that, along with micro entrepreneurs, the executives at Amazon, Chanel or Renault are also thinking...

Do we look good?

Do we sound good?

Do people understand what we are offering?

Are we attracting new customers and keeping loyal ones?

As a micro entrepreneur, you may be thinking, "I've already got a great personality and, I AM my business, so I am my brand. This is easy!" But there is one important difference between our personal brand and our business brand, and that is our customer.

Our customers are the people who are prepared to give us their money and trust in exchange for what we are offering.

For this reason, what our customers need and prefer is more important than what we prefer or think they should accept.

Our brand represents all aspects of our business, so we must listen to our potential customers for that brand to engage them. And not just listen, but also ask questions to ensure what we are offering is really what they want. When it is, not only will they buy, but they will return and tell their friends.

To begin thinking about our business brand the most important question to keep asking ourselves is 'WHY?': "Why am I setting up a business?" and "Why should customers choose me?"

The most successful businesses tap into the 'sweet spot'.

The sweet spot is a meeting of minds between a business and their customers, an alignment of image and perception; communication and understanding; behaviour and response.

This sweet spot is no happy accident. It is found through:

1. **Clearly understanding WHY** we do what we do, **WHAT** exactly we offer, **HOW** we deliver it and the **VALUES** that underpin everything.

And then:

2. **Clearly communicating** that information to people who want what we offer, are attracted to our values and can, therefore, easily understand how we can solve their problems or make their lives easier, more fun, more beautiful or more productive.

To define your business values, we come back to WHY you are in business in the first place. Remember, being good at something is great, but not caring how you do it, or deliver it, will make attracting and keeping customers very hard. For example, if you make beautiful chairs, but you use illegally traded, unsustainable rainforest hardwoods, that is not going to attract people, quite the opposite.

WHY we do what we do may include one or all of the following:

- Expertise

- Passion

- Quality and craftsmanship

- Honesty and care

- Difference

- Belief

- Sustainability

I once heard a micro entrepreneur say: "I can't afford values." In reality, you can't afford NOT to have values.

Values are the roots of your business. Strong brands grow from their values up. When times are tough, going back to your values can save a business.

A business with no values has nothing to save.

With similar values, a business and its customers can build a relationship based on trust and loyalty. It works BOTH ways.

Helping your brand stand out

The brands customers like most are those that offer something others do not. This may be value based and lifestyle based. Whatever sector you are in, you will have competitors: people doing the same kind of business in the same area and, you may think, chasing the same customers.

In 1998 in Taipei, Taiwan, a couple decided to open a café. There were plenty of other cafés in Taipei, thousands in fact. Now, this couple loved cats. They had five of them. They also knew people who were not able to have a pet, so they decided to try something different. They decided to create their café around their cats and share them with their customers.

The Kitten Coffee Garden was the very first 'cat café'. The idea was an instant success and, after a café opened in Japan, the idea quickly spread around the world. The couple were not the first café, or the first café to have cats, but they were the first to put them at the heart of the service they offered. Their brand values were based around caring for animals and generosity to those less fortunate than themselves.

But, this isn't true.

Yes, there will be many businesses similar to yours, BUT they won't be exactly like yours and your opportunity is that they never will be, because you are unique and, therefore, so is your business.

The key is to identify what makes you unique and focus your expertise, values, artistry or knowledge through everything you do. Knowing this will also help you answer another important 'why' question: "Why would a customer choose me?"

For a micro entrepreneur every personal quality you have counts, just as much as the service you are providing and how well you're listening to your customers. All this will go into building your brand.

Your brand will also become more established if you can communicate it easily and professionally with a memorable name, an eye-catching logo and a professional website and marketing materials. Keep in mind:

- Names work best when they are simple.

- Logos work best when they are professionally designed.

- Websites are great tools for supporting all sizes of business but only when they look good and work properly. Again, if you have little expertise, source professional help, you will save yourself time and headaches. The same goes for marketing materials. The key is always to keep it simple.

- Help your customers find you by being where they are looking. When you research your market and type of customer, find out how and where they shop, be that on the Internet, in newspapers and specialist magazines, a shop front or face-to-face appointments. Today, it is likely that you will need to have a presence in a few different places to make an impact.

Top tips for creating a great brand:

- **Be clear on why you are creating your business and why your customer should choose you**

- **Have a good name**

- **Stand for something**

- **Be consistent**

- **Keep your promises**

- **Make yourself easy to find**

- **Be prepared to listen and learn**

Finally, if you get something wrong (and we all do), apologise, learn, make changes and move on. We all make mistakes. It's how we deal with them that will help ensure our brand success.

And remember: fortune favours the brave!

There is an ancient quotation that says, "There is nothing new under the sun." but, there is and it's you. There has never been another 'you' and the world will not see your like again, so, it's time to shine.

Ideas and actions...

"Be Patient.

"Creating
something good
takes time.

"So take your time."

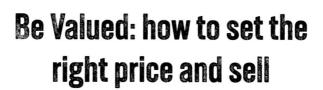

Be Valued: how to set the right price and sell

When we set a price for our product or service, we need to understand three things:

- The COST of what we produce

- Its WORTH or value to our potential customers

- That, whatever we think, ultimately it is our CUSTOMERS that decide what they will pay (and this may be more than you think!)

Costs include your time, materials and expertise. Worth is based on scarcity, customer values and status. Understanding, therefore, your 'ideal customer' is an important part of deciding your price.

In general, when you make or produce something, it would be ideal to sell it for twice what it costs you to buy or make it. For example:

- 50% cost of production – materials, tools, rent, wages

- 50% profit

When you sell services, for example consultancy, accounting, translation, copywriting or legal help, your price calculation may be based on a basic hourly rate to cover:

- % for fixed costs, such as office, travel, equipment, software

- % for your time

- % for profit

However, market factors will affect the basic price of any product or service. These are:

1. Your competitors' prices

and, more importantly,

2. What you or your product is worth to your customer – your common values, your experience and how special, unique or rare you are.

Know your worth

If you are the only plumber in town, your prices are going to be higher than if there were 20 others to choose from. This is because your worth to the residents of the town, over and above the actual cost of what you do, is very high. Your worth would also be high if there were 20 other plumbers but you were the only one who knew how to fix a leaking tap.

If you offer professional or intellectual services, and, for example, you are the only accountant in town your fees will follow a similar pattern to the plumber, based on scarcity and unique skills.

People will pay more for what they value, such as:

Expertise

Experience

Quality

Trustworthiness

Uniqueness and exclusivity

People also prefer to choose a business with shared personal values, for example: family business, eco-friendly, etc.

Your worth to your customer increases with every value you share... It's like 'speaking their language'.

It's important to look at your business from you customers' point of view. What would build their trust, add value and help you stand out from your competitors? How about:

- An unique product

- Personalised delivery

- Free tasters

- After-sales support

- Multi-buy discount

- Money-back guarantee

- Qualifications and accreditations

- Testimonials

- Brand values

- Niche expertise and experience

How you present yourself and how you behave also has a big impact on people's perception and trust of your business. We look at this aspect in B*e noticed: How to create a great brand* and also *Be Seen: How to develop your website and marketing materials*.

Let's face it, if the broken, hand-painted sign hung on your gate looks like your five-year-old son painted it, no one could be blamed for giving your flying lessons a miss.

Finally, test and measure your price. Don't be afraid to make a change if something isn't working. It is always wise to: "fail fast and move on."

How to be good at selling things

Most people I talk to don't like selling things. It makes them feel awkward and anxious.

As a micro entrepreneur and startup business, your 'sales team' is probably just you and, if you are lucky, one other. So feeling anxious about 'selling' is not healthy when no sales mean no business.

If you do feel anxious about selling, stop thinking about a 'sale'. Breathe and start thinking about how you can help people and build trust. Ask yourself the questions: "Who can I help, where are they and how can I help them find me easily?"

Sales take trust and trust takes time

As a startup you won't have a well-known reputation or brand to help persuade customers to buy from you, so an important first step on the road to building sales is building trust.

Think for a moment. How long would you want to know someone before you would be happy to lend them money?

Would you feel happy lending money to someone you only know a little? How about someone you have just met? How about someone you have never met?

You are asking people you have never met to give you money – to trust you. That is why building and maintaining trust with your customers is an essential part of building a successful business. Trust and good relationships rely on:

- Generosity
- Reliability
- Support
- Honesty
- Consistency
- Credibility
- Response

When you think about growing a relationship, not simply 'making a sale', you will find that your potential customer may not buy from you immediately, but they will begin to trust you. They will be comfortable asking your advice. They will remember you and, importantly, they will buy from you and are more likely to recommend you to others.

Stop talking... Start listening

Whatever it is that you provide, from a holiday home to art classes, accountancy or hairdressing to building services, before you can begin selling you need to listen to your potential customers and observe your competitors.

Spending time finding out how others market and deliver their services or products is a great way to spot a gap or a new opportunity. It will help you understand what is

Tell your story...

Le Moulin de Pensol is an old mill. Nestling in the hilly folds and forests of the Haute Vienne region of southwest France, it's home to British owners Heidi and Nik, and its barns and outbuildings bring in income as charming holiday gîtes. The surrounding land covers some eight hectares of pasture, woods, streams and meadows with paths radiating out to join the miles of national forest tracks. An area popular with British, Dutch and French holidaymakers, there are plenty of similar properties and competition to attract guests. Le Moulin de Pensol's growing reputation and bookings are because of why and how Heidi and Nik have chosen to sell their particular brand of holiday.

Heidi and Nik focus on sharing their love of wildlife and nature: flowers, insects, donkey-grazed pastures, tame pigs and sustainability. Blogs focus on the seasons and what you can find growing, burrowing or flying by. With 61 species of butterfly to spot on their land alone, they advertise in nature and butterfly conservation magazines, as well as the more usual places. They appeal to people who already have an interest or are actively looking for time out in nature and an ecological approach to living. For customers looking for this type of holiday, it is not 'if', but, 'when' can we book?

different about what you offer, as well as giving you some good ideas.

Be seen regularly and often

Selling is also about being seen. Find out where your customers get their information. Is it from the Internet, from the local paper, a specialist magazine or on the high street? It is also worth getting out into your local community to talk about what you do and why. Think about any interest and business groups or specialist clubs.

Your story can also often be more powerful than a list of service features. Why and how you came to be in business is another part of your sales toolkit that you can draw on to engage people emotionally. Many micro entrepreneurs use a blog or speaking event to build up an audience that will turn into their customer base.

Being able to sell is not just about what we sell and where, but also how we sell it. Read *Be Noticed: How to Create a Great Brand* for more advice on brand building.

Don't undersell yourself – how to negotiate

If you offer professional services, as opposed to a set price product, whether it's an hourly rate or a flat fee, don't begin any negotiation with the price, or introduce it before the client does. Instead introduce all the reasons they should choose you, for example: your aptitude and experience for the subject matter; your resources; your ability to deliver in their timeframe and your shared values. In this way you have the opportunity to build trust.

People care less about the cost when they have peace of mind

If the client does bring up price first, simply request more information, because how can you quote properly before you understand their requirements? Resist the urge or pressure to give a quote on the spot. Give yourself time to think about it, tell them when you'll respond and ensure you get back to them, as promised, with your considered estimate.

If clients want a discount what's in it for you? Are they offering a long-term project where regular work would help you out? Will it help get your business off the ground and help build up your reviews? Reducing your fees can mean you agree to take out a certain activity and still satisfy your client. When you give away your time and expertise for free, some people will be happy to keep taking; they don't value you or your time and are not the clients you want. Remember to always reflect any discounts on the invoice or within the contract.

Finally, it is wise to state on any quote that should their requirements change during the project, then, so will your fees. Reassure them that when this happens you will discuss it with them. This helps avoid you doing more work than was originally agreed.

"Wishing to be friends is quick work, but friendship is a slow ripening fruit."

Aristotle
Greek philosopher and polymath, 384–322 BCE

Integrity and reputation

When we first talk to our customers, it can be very tempting to show off all the benefits and features of something we are trying to sell, but it's important not to over promise or exaggerate. Remember: your voice is not the important one in the relationship. When your customers feel listened to, when they can get all their questions answered and they feel valued, their loyalty, trust and wallet will follow. When you negotiate, be confident, clear and consistent. Now is the time to remind them how much easier their lives will be if they choose you!

You won't build an empire with one advert, one blog post or one conversation, but, if you make a choice to do the best you can every day with what you have and who you know, without fail, becoming good at sales can be as simple, and as powerful, as that.

Top tips for how to set the right price and sell:

- Look like you mean business
- Take a deep breath, this is a marathon not a sprint
- Think about how best to help people and build trust
- Listen to your customers and learn from your competitors
- Understand what your customers value
- Understand your own worth and negotiate with confidence
- Be consistent
- Be found

Being honest and authentic comes down to one thing:

"You are what you do. Not what you say you'll do."

Carl Jung
Swiss psychiatrist and founder of analytical psychology.

Ideas and actions...

Be Seen: how to develop your marketing plan

If you have something to sell, you need to be easy to see, find and engage with.

Once we have defined our brand and set our price, we need to make sure our business is visible, attractive and approachable. We need a plan!

A business without marketing is a hobby and hobbies don't pay the rent. So what now?

Good marketing is a very important element of building a successful business and here's how to make a great start...

Look at the marketing of different businesses you use both large and small. What do you like? What do you dislike? Can you work out why?

Now look at your direct competitors. People with the same kind of business as you, in your area. Again, what do you like and dislike about their marketing? Do you know why?

Whatever your competitors are doing, your job is to do it better.

Today, the successful marketing of any product or service requires a mixture of things. For a micro business that mix may include:

Printed marketing

- Business card
- Brochure
- Leaflet
- Newspaper advert
- Magazine article
- Press release

Online (or digital) marketing

- Personal website
- Social media, for example: YouTube, Instagram, X, Facebook
- Blog
- 'Marketplace' website, for example: eBay, Etsy, Amazon
- Professional platform website, for example: LinkedIn or a membership or accredited organisation

Human to human

- Word of mouth
- Personal connections
- Professional networking

The different elements that make up your 'marketing mix' should be chosen by understanding your customers' buying habits, so do your research. When you have identified how your customers hear about the kind of product you offer and how and where they shop for it, it's time to set some goals, create a plan and decide on your marketing mix.

Set Your goals

Short-term, mid-term and long-term. Your goals will change as you develop your business, but without goals you cannot keep focussed on what you want to achieve or measure your success.

For example, your goals may be:

> **Short:** Secure a business loan from my bank or start a blog.

> **Mid:** Secure ten clients by the end of six months or buy special equipment.

> **Long:** Employ five staff and open four outlets by the end of three years.

Or, more simply, "To pay my bills and give me the lifestyle and freedom I want."

Everyone's goals and timescales will be different, but they are all important. Now to make a plan...

"A goal without a plan is just a wish..."

Antoine De Saint-Exupéry
French writer, poet and pioneering aviator.

Create a plan to reach your goals

Think of your plan as a series of stepping stones to reach your goal.

If you are crossing a deep river, without stepping stones it will be difficult, if not impossible, to make progress. For example:

Plan to reach your short-term goal to secure a business loan

1. Get advice from local business support service.

2. Write draft business plan.

3. Make appointment with bank.

Mid-term goal to secure ten clients by end of six months:

1. Research local advertising and competitors.

2. Research website resources and support.

3. Begin creating content and images for advert and website.

You get the picture? Each goal has a plan attached with different stages within it. Reaching your short-, mid- and long-term goals will also go on simultaneously and many may overlap.

Build your marketing mix to support your plan and achieve your goals.

Use your plan to keep you on track

For example, if you offer yoga classes, your marketing mix may include:

Printed

- Leaflets for local community spaces
- Adverts in the local newspaper and/or wellbeing magazine

Online

- Website
- Facebook page
- YouTube Channel

Human

- Encourage word of mouth through meeting up with local interest groups
- Who do you know and who do they know? Use your personal networks and connections to spread the word.

When creating any type of marketing remember:

1. People want to know the benefits to them before anything else.

2. Reflect what your customer wants or needs to know, not what you want to tell them (see point 1)

3. Ensure your brand (name, logo, presentation) is professional, attractive and consistent.

4. Make it easy for people to find and contact you.

Most importantly, review what you are doing regularly and, when needed, change your plan and your marketing mix not your goal.

Now, let's take a quick look at content and design, in other words: what your marketing material says and how it looks.

Part of building trust with your customer will be choosing the right language and tone of voice. This may depend on what you sell: hairdressing or legal services, car maintenance or fashion design. Choose the tone of voice and language appropriate to your customers. This will make them feel at ease. We look at this in more detail in our guide *Be Persuasive: how to advertise*.

If you want to engage customers from different countries in different languages, read our free Translation Guides and get help with translation. AI translation services like Google Translate will never be as good, as accurate or as sensitive as a human. Again, it comes back to trust. Ensure you are talking about and selling your products and services in the most authentic and engaging way you can to help build your customers' trust and loyalty.

When it comes to designing a logo and the look of a leaflet or website, it's also important to get the 'visual language' right. This applies to pictures, colours and text design. If you don't have design skills, get professional help. Whatever budget you have, maximise it by hiring the best professional help you can. If you have little money to spend, just **KEEP IT SIMPLE.**

And remember, before printing, publishing or posting anything, ask someone else to read it first to spot any mistakes. If you are on your own, put it to one side and re-read it later.

Finally...

> **Question:** What is the most common mistake people make when producing their first marketing materials?

> **Answer:** They forget to include their contact details.

Ideas and actions...

Be Seen Online: how to develop a good website

Today, the Internet offers us a wonderful way to talk to the world.

As well as a website to showcase what we do, there are also a range of professional networking websites, such as LinkedIn, and marketplace websites, including Etsy, Amazon, Ebay, Airbnb and Booking.com, to name just a few popular ones.

As well as having your own website, this wide range of digital platforms offers a micro entrepreneur or business startup lots of ways to promote and sell their services and products around the world.

I regularly get asked, "Do I really need a website?" and 99 times out of 100 my answer is, "Yes."

I also get asked, "Do I need to sign up to all the popular social media platforms like Facebook, X, Instagram, YouTube and TikTok?" My answer is always, "No", what you DO NEED to do is find out where and in which ways your customers are shopping online. When you know this, THEN you can focus your time and efforts on those specific social platforms and not waste your time on the others.

In this guide we are focussing on how to develop a good website and we will look at social media in more detail in our guide, *Be Heard: how to get results from social media.*

So, should everyone have a website?

For a homeowner with a room to rent, or someone with a parking space to let, marketplace websites like Airbnb are perfect as they help people raise a little cash.

For people renting out a whole villa, cottage, gîte, traditional bed and breakfast, or a valet and parking service, which will generate substantially higher taxable income, it becomes a business. And, as a business, you need to attract a steady flow of customers and do need your own website.

For lots of small businesses, using a marketplace website like Amazon is a key part of their marketing mix. However, it is also very wise to have your own website where you can fully promote what you do. This may include lots of additional product or service information; being able to engage your customers by telling your story, offering discounts and sharing know-how; and, importantly, being independent of a marketplace website that you have no control over.

It is also a question of trust

In our marketing guides we talk about building trust. It should come as no surprise that building customer trust is the job of your website too.

Many customers who come across you on a marketplace website will look for your personal website link or make a separate Internet search for you. They do this because they want to be sure they are making a good buying decision: that you are who you say you are and that you can be trusted. Many people also prefer to make direct contact to benefit from direct discounts, but mostly for peace of mind.

A good website builds trust and trust will build your business.

A poor website damages trust and your reputation.

Here are the basic requirements for a good website:

- Working – all pages can be read with no broken links

- Readable – is easy to read, understand and navigate

- Visible – can be viewed on a desktop, tablet or mobile phone

- Informative – gives the information your customer wants and needs

- Actionable – allows visitors to take action, for example, to contact you, book or buy

- Searchable* – can be found by the main search engines, like Google, Bing and Yahoo

When you develop your website ensure that you can also access information on your 'web traffic'. Web traffic describes how many people find your site and what they do when they get there. You can use the free tool Google Analytics to check how many people are visiting, where they come from, what pages they are reading, how long they are spending on the site, and which pages they exit from. Use this feedback to help you improve your website content over time.

*A good website should be built, not only to give visitors what they want, but also to attract the Internet search engines that will list it. This depends on a clean, well-organised site structure, well-written content, together with search engine optimised (SEO) text and images. Ensuring these things will give your website the best chance of being listed by search engines. We will look at SEO in more detail later.

The golden rule: "keep it simple" and...

1. Make your website your 'mothership', your online 'hub', and use your marketing mix and social media to drive people to it.

2. On every page create a 'call to action' telling visitors what they can do, for example: 'buy here', 'find us', 'see more' and 'get in touch'. Don't think they will automatically know what to do. In fact assume that they won't.

3. Make contacting you easy with a very visible phone number, email address or online contact form.

4. Give people plenty of reasons to return. For example, insightful blogs, free resources and 'how to' articles – be helpful, it will build trust.

5. If you know how to build and develop a website, great! If you don't, save yourself time, energy and your customers' trust by seeking help from professionals.

Be wary of 'free' website design and hosting offers. They seem like fantastic value at first but look closer...

'Free' usually means your website will show other companies adverts. It might load slowly, which will frustrate your visitors. This is usually with the aim of getting you to sign up to a monthly payment plan to achieve a better service.

It may only offer very limited functions, which you will find hard to change.

You may not be able to move your website away from the free host. Read all the terms and conditions carefully.

It is always wise to speak to a reputable website business, who should not ask you to pay for an introductory chat or pressure you into joining them.

If you do want to take advantage of a free hosting deal, do your research to find the best terms for your circumstances.

When it comes to pictures, colours, layout and text, if you don't have design skills, get professional help. Whatever budget you have, maximise it by hiring the best help you can. The 'visual language' of marketing is very important and we will look at this in *Be Persuasive: how to advertise*. This is worth knowing because it absolutely applies to a website!

Don't be put off!

"The most courageous act is still to think for yourself. Aloud."

Coco Chanel
Founder and namesake of the Chanel brand.

There are currently around 200 million active websites on the World Wide Web today*. But, don't be put off. People are looking for what you offer.

*internetlivestats.com

Rome wasn't built in a day and neither was anyone's Internet presence.

It takes time for search engines to find your site, check its contents and index it. It takes time and effort for you to build trust and an online audience.

A picture is worth a thousand words

Fonsegre is a wonderful, spacious farmhouse chambre d'hôte with bed and breakfast and gîtes set in the rolling fields of Burgundy, close to the walled medieval market town of Nevers. A working farm, Fonsegre is also a haven for travellers on the N7 and visitors to the historic Magny Cours racetrack and is owned and run by a Franco-British couple David and Isabel. Quietly emerging from Fonsegre's many attractions are Isabel's creative cooking, superb dishes and her love of good ingredients.

Beautifully created and presented, Isabel's seasonal dishes are always a delightful addition to a stay. Few, if any, guests leave without applauding the cook! You'll find Isabel's dishes showcased on her website and Instagram feeds. Despite being neither a professional photographer, nor a chef, Isabel's lovingly designed and prepared dishes are a great example of using a personal passion to engage customers and attract recommendations and new visitors. Her stylish food also sets the tone for the simply, yet lovingly, decorated rooms and spaces.

A website can be a great showcase, resource and sales tool, BUT it's just a bunch of pixels without visitors. Through all the different elements of your marketing mix, you should be driving people towards your website and this activity needs to be regular and consistent.

People are busy. They make thousands of decisions every day. Your job is to make finding and using your website one of the easy ones.

A last word about photographs and other images...

Today's mobile phones are capable of taking and editing superb photographs and videos. It is worth practising. Think about light, angle, different filters and interest for the viewer.

If you are photographing products, keep the backgrounds plain and ensure good lighting and a range of angles.

For other images, if you are not confident enough to use your own photography, you can find and download thousands of good quality photographs on page 215. You'll find information on a wide range of free image libraries, along with tips on how to get the most from these resources, file size and copyright issues Free Image Library. If you need very specific imagery, seek professional help and never randomly download images from the Internet without permission from the photographer. It may feel like an easy and quick solution, but you may attract the wrong kind of attention!

Ideas and actions...

Be Persuasive: how to advertise

Choose the right words and pictures

Persuading someone to buy from you takes two key things.

The first is to talk and write in their 'language'. Not just their native tongue (although this is a huge help!), it's about using the right words, images and tone of voice to attract people looking for what you are selling.

The second part is to reinforce their buying decision by making them feel it's a good choice, whether that means they feel:

younger

richer

stronger

wiser

greener

prettier

cleaner

smarter

happier

more organised

more fashionable… or, maybe just more fun!

Not including your grocery shopping, what was the last thing you bought? Why did you choose that in particular? What influenced you? Do you remember how you felt when you bought it?

Science!

Deep within our brains is the amygdala. Part of the limbic system, this area has been identified by neuroscientists as governing our emotions, as well as playing a role in decision making.

So if you want to persuade someone to buy something, you need to think about how to influence the way they will **FEEL** about making that decision.

You want them to feel good enough to make it a habit.

Successful persuasion is not just about WHAT we say, it's also HOW we say it and WHY.

Combining visual signals AND emotional response.

Think back to our branding guide and the importance of understanding why you are in business. If you don't understand your motivation – your values and what sets you apart from your competitors – how is anyone else going to know?

The 'why' of your business should sit at the heart of your advertising. It will help you engage and build trust, and make an easy buying decision for your customers.

In fact, everything you do as a business plays a role in persuading your customers to choose you. **EVERYTHING**.

When we persuade our customers to buy from us, they are placing their trust in us to deliver. When we deliver on our promises, we can build loyalty and a good reputation.

Before modern print advertising arrived in the 15th century with the invention of the printing press, ancient Egyptians created papyrus posters; Romans painted their walls; others used song, poetry and stories to advertise. Since the 15th century, by and large, nothing much changed until the invention of the postal service, radio, film, television and, today, the Internet. What makes the Internet a phenomenal sales tool is that anyone with an Internet connection can advertise, not just to their town or region, but to the world. Some with much more success than others, and here's why.

When we read information, two things happen:

1. The words create pictures in our minds (visual)

2. We feel attracted or repelled (emotional)

Both these things happen within milliseconds and repeat thousands of times a day as we are bombarded by a near-constant flow of information and advertising all around us. Even when we look for something we really want, and are more focussed on what we are reading, the process is the same.

When we see a picture, our brains respond even faster.

That's because our brains process images much faster than words, especially if our reading skills are poor or we are reading an unfamiliar language. It is true what they say, "A picture is worth a thousand words" and we process the information much faster too.

Now we know why it is worth getting BOTH the words and pictures we use to promote and persuade right. It's a powerful combination, so, let's look at the words first.

The key to successful persuasion – using the right words to advertise

Along with ensuring that you are using the right tone of voice for your customers, if you remember nothing else, remember this: people are only interested in themselves.

Whether it is donating to a charity, or buying the latest iPhone, it will be THEIR interests and THEIR beliefs that drive that buying decision. Think of this as their VALUES.

The key to successful persuasion is being able to match all the **BENEFITS** you offer to your customer's **VALUES**, supported by evidence to build trust.

For your printed advertising, website or social media, matching the benefits of what you offer to customers' values is a good way to work out what persuasive words and images would work best.

A housebuilder

Customer Benefits		Customer Values
Safety certificates	⟶	Qualifications
Multiple languages	⟶	Easy communication
Local	⟶	Buy local
Free quotations	⟶	Builds trust
Client testimonial	⟶	**Evidence** to build trust
Guaranteed work	⟶	**Evidence** to build trust

A rural holiday home

Customer Benefits	Customer Values
Countryside location ⟶	Peace and quiet
Solar panels ⟶	Sustainability
Pets allowed ⟶	Animal lover
Close to leisure lake ⟶	Outdoor activities
Guest reviews ⟶	**Evidence** to build trust

Let's look at the example of an advert for a yoga class. The yoga studio owner has done their research into the type of customer they want to attract: they are young people working in the city centre; they like to feel good, but may be nervous of trying something new. The yoga studio owner needs to match all the benefits of their yoga classes to their new customers' values and support this with evidence.

The advert is constructed to appeal directly to these new customers, telling them what they want to hear by aligning with their values.

The advert:

1. Reassures them.

2. Appeals to them.

3. Gives them good reasons to sign up.

4. Builds trust.

5. Shows them an image of what they could feel like – a happy, healthy, relaxed person that they can relate to.

6. Asks for action and makes it easy to get in contact or find out more.

Improve your health and wellbeing

Welcome to our friendly multi-lingual Yoga City sessions.

Open to all, our qualified, experienced teachers will guide you every step of the way in our relaxed and refreshing classes.

It's easy to learn and we're easy to find in our central city location!

Get 50% off your first class or bring a friend with you for free.

"Yoga City gives me the best start to my day, everyday!"
Kim B

Call 123 456 78 or email
to book your place today!

YOGA CITY – *your health, your way*

namaste@yogacity.studio

The yoga class

Customer Benefits:

- Proven health benefits
- City centre location
- Qualified instructors
- Different levels of classes
- Starter discount/bring a friend for free
- Customer testimonial

Customer Values:

- Would like to be healthier
- Wants somewhere close to work
- Prefers qualified teachers
- Wants reassurance on choice
- Is careful with money
- Needs reassurance

Think about your business and how you can match all the benefits you offer to your target customers' values to attract them.

We can't all be great at photography. Thankfully, there are websites that offer royalty-free pictures. In other words, you can use them in your advertising and on your website and social media for free without fees or a licence.

Discover high-quality pictures from around the world on all kinds of subjects taken by some very talented photographers.

Have a look at our Free Image Library chapter for royalty-free, licence-free photography and graphics for advertising and websites.

Finally … something to keep in mind: to be persuasive and advertise anything, be anything you want, but don't be boring!

When you want to advertise, take the time to make your words and pictures stand out and you can persuade people to choose you.

"Your business is only as successful as the number of customers you manage to persuade."

Bushra Azhar
Best-selling author of Mass Persuasion Method.

Ideas and actions...

Be Heard: how to get results from social media

Social media hands us a microphone to help amplify our ideas and messages throughout our regions, countries and around the world.

Social media is also an opportunity to connect and learn from others outside our personal networks. Here's how to start getting results.

Social media is free to use for anyone with an Internet connection. Download the app and away you go... Great free promotion!

But hang on... Social media can be a lot of work for little reward UNLESS you research, target and plan your activity. To enjoy successful social media you need a good social media strategy.

"Everything connects"

Leonardo da Vinci
Sculptor, engineer, scientist, artist 1452–1519.

Working out a social media strategy...

Today, the most popular social media platforms include: Facebook, Instagram, YouTube, Pinterest, LinkedIn and TikTok with new ones emerging all the time. You probably have your own personal favourites.

Being in business, however, is different. It does not mean we must automatically use social media. Beware people who say: "You MUST be on Facebook..." or, "What! You're not on TikTok?"

Your business social media should not be about personal preferences, following the latest trend, or what a well-meaning friend might say. Business social media should be focussed on our customers' and clients' preferences: what platforms they use, what they respond to and want to know.

Some people who set up in business rush to sign up to a range of social media accounts. They spend too much time posting at random and quickly become frustrated because they don't get the results they expected, saying, "Social media is a waste of time! It doesn't work..." And they are right. For them social media won't work because they don't understand what they are doing or have a strategy to get results.

In order to create the right social media strategy and make the best use of your time and effort, you need to start by getting clear on your needs, expectations and goals. For the Micro Oiseau translation project we asked ourselves these questions, so, here to help you, we've supplied our answers.

1.   Why do you want to use social media?

"We want people to get to know and trust us. We want to promote what we do. We want people to find us easily. Remember: trust is a huge part of the buying process."

2.   What results do you want from social media?

"We want to build an audience of like-minded people, a community that will choose us for trusted information and translator referrals over a competitor when they are ready to buy. Forget fast sales, social media requires patience and strategy."

3.   Which apps are you going to choose and why?

"We'll focus on:

- LinkedIn for business startup groups, entrepreneurs, professional translators, and referrals

- Facebook for translator groups and small business owners

- Instagram for small business community, ambitious entrepreneurs and startups around the world."

Focus your efforts where you will find most of your customers...

If you have a dog-grooming service Facebook, Instagram and YouTube offer great visual showcases for what you do. Think about it. Most people will not visit YouTube to find an accountant.

If you are an accountant look for interest groups across LinkedIn and Facebook and join in the conversations. With its largest user group aged from 18 to 24, TikTok shouldn't be your first thought!

If you are an artist or musician, think about how and where art and music fans go to find inspiration and share. These may include, YouTube, Instagram and TikTok.

If you discover that your customers use little or no social media, then you would be a busy fool if you decided you had to! But remember, if your products or services are for the very young or very old, although they might not use social media, their families and influencers will.

Monitor engagement and response, and change what you do depending on your results.

4. What are you going to share, and why?

> "We will share great free marketing guides and business support. We will showcase talented translators through different languages, high-quality profiles and Google rankings. We will repost information of interest and signpost services, we will encourage and engage."

What you share should be guided by your customer research and always in line with your values or brand behaviour. It needs to focus on your customers' needs. In this way you will build trust, engage and signpost them to your website.

Websites are where buying decisions are made, so don't forget to add your link to your posts!

5. How much time should you spend on social media?

> "We're going to dedicate time every week to create content, schedule posts and review results."

Social media can be a hungry monster and it takes time to build an audience. Keep in mind this is a marathon not a sprint and, unless you can pay a social media company to create and run campaigns for you, the best advice is to forget quick results. Your route to success is about making your social media a habit through a realistic and regular posting schedule. Post content that will attract and engage the customers you want; use one platform well, not three badly. Later in our guide we look at post frequency.

Tip: how to find like-minded people

To find groups of people talking about and sharing content on a particular subject, use a hashtag #.

Hashtags are used in social media posts like subject labels and they help people find content they are interested in, for example: #translation, #holidays #vegan. You can perform a hashtag search on each social media platform to find ones that are currently popular and/or useful to you. You can also make up your own, using it each time you post. It's important not to use too many. Two to four is ideal on most social media platforms, however, Instagram is different and allows up to 30.

Another good tip is to use capital letters in a word string. This ensures that screen reading technology used by partially sighted or blind people can identify the individual words. For example: #MarketingGuides.

Using hashtags in your posts will help people find you and share your content.

Social media is a good way to begin a conversation.

And conversations are about listening, just as much as talking.

It is always best to listen first, so, as you work out your strategy take your time. I can guarantee that no one is holding their breath for you. Follow your competitors, people you admire, organisations you trust and brands you like. Support them by reposting their content. This will also give you some good ideas about how to create your own content.

Ideas to help you get started

Through your branding and sales preparation, you will have identified some unique things about your product or service, so focus on these to interest an audience that thinks like you and...

1. **Forget heavy sales messages**. It is OK to share a special or seasonal offer once in a while but don't simply keep saying, "please buy me, buy me, buy me". No one likes to be told what to do, you need to talk about the BENEFITS you offer and give reasons WHY someone should give you a second look.

2. **Develop the habit to help, inspire and inform. Here's a handy reminder to help spark ideas for posts**:

   - Value – content that is useful, full of ideas and information

   - Currency – content that delivers news and trends

   - Story – content that inspires, like your brand story

   - Emotion – content that taps into desire, joy, fun and fear (but less of fear!)

3. **Avoid unprofessional content, this includes:**

   - Being unkind or negative about people and cultures

   - Repeating unverified information

   - Offering political opinion (leave this to your personal social media)

   - Offering religious opinion (seasonal greetings are fine but, unless you are a religious leader, again, it is unwise)

   - Swear words

4. If you receive a comment or a message try to respond as soon as you can, or within 24 hours.

If you receive a complaint or a criticism (allow yourself to be irritated, then calm down) respond politely and quickly: apologise for any inconvenience and ask them to discuss the matter with you offline and give them a way to do this via contact details on your website or a private direct message (DM). Do not respond to them in any other way online. This approach ensures you and your business are not involved in a potentially harmful public argument. Importantly, whatever the issue, you and your follower can resolve it privately without an audience.

Remember: complaints are always more valuable than praise.

You also now have an opportunity to turn the situation around and talk about how you can improve what you do.

Tip

Check in with your website Google Analytics to see which social media platforms are feeding visitors to your website. This will help you refine your social media calendar and marketing mix.

How often to post on social media

You now know WHY you want to use social media, WHAT you want to post and on WHICH platform. It is time to create a social media calendar as part of your marketing mix to identify WHEN and HOW OFTEN.

Check out our free resources for a flexible template to do just that.

Keep your output regular and consistent

Review regularly to see when you get a reaction and adjust as necessary. You may also like to investigate social media scheduling tools like Hootsuite and Buffer that can offer time savings with 'dashboards' displaying all your streams and posts in one place. You will find a wide range of free and fee-based options to choose from.

Setting time aside in the week to sit down and schedule posts can help you achieve your goals. There is no magic formula for frequency. It depends on your product and audience.

Top Tips for a successful social media strategy

1. Do your customer research.

2. Be clear on the results you want with the resources you have.

3. Start slowly, listen and learn.

4. Create your strategy.

5. Be consistent.

6. Fill in your social media profiles fully, using high-quality images, consistent branding and language that reflects your website. This will help ensure that you are recognisable, memorable and professional.

7. Engage with others and share.

8. Keep control of your social accounts. If someone else posts for you, ENSURE you keep ownership and login details. Because, if that person disappears so will your social media assets.

9. Be patient and creative with your content. Let your personality shine through. People love doing business with people they trust.

And finally...

10. Importantly, make your social media useful and support others.

Use your knowledge and experience to help others. Share the beautiful, interesting, funny and informative. Your values, what you do and how you do it will attract people and when they find you, make sure you drive them towards to your website. If you do this, then social media can do a great job for your business, and earn its keep.

"Generosity is a wonderful introduction."

Ideas and actions...

Be Professional: how to make a great first impression

As a business owner, micro entrepreneur and professional in your field, it is important to look and sound good; to be able to speak clearly and intelligently about what you do and the ideas you have in an authentic way. Making a good first impression will help sustain and promote trust in you your products, services and, of course, your brand.

"You never get a second chance to make a first impression."

Will Rogers
American's 'favourite cowboy' Native American actor and social commentator.

When we start a business we will find ourselves in front of people.

We might be:

- Meeting

- Presenting

- Pitching

Being the focus of attention, however, can be uncomfortable. Talking to people about ourselves, our ideas and services, be it two or 200, is not easy, especially given the pressure of knowing that how accomplished we are has a direct impact on our brand and business prospects.

For this reason, no time or effort to improve our engagement and presentation skills is ever wasted. It can also have a positive impact on our wider lives.

Look good – what people see

Professionals should look, professional!

Within every trade and sector there is usually an acceptable way to dress. Think of lawyers, dentists, builders or yoga teachers. All very different. These may be traditions that you are keen to change. If so, great! It may help you stand out from your competitors. How you present yourself should be part of your wider brand and it's completely your choice. BUT whatever you choose to wear there are some universal truths when you want to attract and engage others.

You have to look like you care…

1. Look fresh

2. Smell good

3. Smile – there has never been and will never be a better way to engage another human being than a smile. It's hard not to return!

When you take care of your appearance, others will take note.

Sound good – what people hear

To capture people's attention here are three top things to think about when talking to people face-to-face.

1. **Breathe –** use breathing exercises before you begin to calm your nerves, slow your heart rate, control your voice, clear your mind and relax your body. *You will find an easy-to-follow breathing exercise later in this guide.*

2. **Open up –** crossing your arms or holding them tightly to your sides is your body language signalling, "I'm not comfortable and not approachable"and when we are nervous it is a natural defence mechanism to stand or sit this way. To prevent this, breathe, drop your shoulders and loosen up your arms by bending them slightly at the elbow. If it helps, clasp a few fingers lightly in front of you until you feel more relaxed. When talking it's good to use gestures but keep them light and varied. Don't point. Pointing can be seen as aggressive, it's better to keep an open hand signalling transparency.

3. **Slow down –** if there is one thing that instantly improves our speech and delivery it is to simply slow down.. It's also about pace and building in "understanding space" around important facts, figures and ideas. Don't be afraid of moments of silence like these. A pause before or after a key piece of information can be very powerful because it:

   • Allows your listener to process what you are saying

   • Displays your confidence and builds trust

   • Gives you a chance to breathe and a moment to decide what to say next!

Speak authentically – what you say

When you have got people's attention, it's time to tell them what they want to know, or, better still, what they didn't think they wanted to know but now find completely fascinating.

Here are the top tips for speaking with authority and authenticity:

1. **Be yourself –** it's less exhausting and you won't slip up.

2. **Adapt what you say to your audience –** the size, their interest and prior knowledge.

3. **Don't use jargon –** it won't make you sound clever. Your audience will simply lose interest and think you're arrogant.

4. **Don't use three words when one will do –** you will just get tangled up and trip over your own thoughts.

5. **Be confident –** but don't lie or embellish the facts. You'll get found out.

6. **Show your passion –** people love people who love what they do. If you think it's better to be 'cool' see point three.

Now, let's look at a situation where our breathing can make all the difference to our vocal and verbal delivery. Imagine the scene...

You are standing in front of an audience who are waiting for you to say something.

You are nervous and your body is tense.

Your tension makes your mouth dry and your voice sound shallow and weak, or perhaps, uncontrolled and too loud.

Your brain feels 'foggy' and you forget to talk about some key information.

You become frustrated because you know you are not getting your message across.

Your audience senses your difficulty and becomes restless.

Now everybody is uncomfortable and anxious.

But don't despair! There are a number of easy-to-learn techniques to dispel stress, calm nerves and make sure that your audience not only listens to what you have to say, but will stay with you to the end.

The key is in how we breathe

Harnessing our breath

As well as our lungs, our breath feeds our brains with oxygen to help us concentrate and, via our blood, it feeds our muscles to keep us upright.

BUT

In order for our breath to help reduce our levels of stress it takes thought and practice to slow down the heart rate, calm the nerves and clear the brain. Before you are due to speak, take a moment to:

- Stand up straight – if sitting, sit up and centred

- Head looking forward with a relaxed jaw

- Relax your shoulders and let them drop away from your ears

- Plant your feet firmly on the ground
- Do not lock your knees

Now breathe slowly and deeply IN through your nose and OUT through your mouth.

As you breath in imagine the air flowing IN via your belly button filling the lower part of your lungs first.

Once your lungs are full breathe OUT slowly through the mouth, emptying the lungs over a slow count of 10.

Repeat this process trying to increase the out breath count gradually to 12, then 15 or even 20.

The more often you practise this technique the sooner you'll have a natural and effective way of calming your nerves. As a result when you need to speak your voice will sound strong, your body will have less tension, your mind will be clear and you'll look and sound confident.

Opportunities for small business owners and micro entrepreneurs can come from unexpected places so it always pays to be prepared with some thoughts to share. And, just like in our guide *Be Valued: how to set the right price and sell*, don't think about a 'sale'. Think about building a relationship and when talking to anyone keep in mind:

- Who you can help
- How you can help

And, of course, smile and breath!

"Breath is the link between mind and body."

Dan Brulé

Pioneer in breathwork, author, coach and trainer.

Ideas and actions...

Be Professional Online: how to prepare for virtual meetings

Meeting online is a good business option for many small businesses and micro entrepreneurs, especially for home workers or those in different time zones, in isolated locations or with mobility issues.

COVID19 and the necessity for social distancing meant that millions more were introduced to software including Zoom, WhatsApp, FaceTime, Messenger, Telegram, Microsoft Teams and Skype. It's not surprising that the virtual meeting is here to stay and, in some cases, may be the best option. So it's important to be as prepared, professional and productive as possible for your virtual or online meetings.

Many people have found that online meetings can help boost as well as offering greater flexibility and wider collaboration, so knowing how to make the most of any virtual opportunity is important for entrepreneurs and businesses.

The best way to be productive is to be prepared.

In this guide we're going to look at the best way to:

- Be a great host

- Be a great attendee

- Make the best use of the time allowed

- Confidently contribute

- Build trust with a personal, yet always professional, approach

Get to know the software or application

When you have been invited to host or join an online meeting you need to ensure that you are comfortable with the software or application you are going to use. Although the different applications all do a similar job, there are some differences. Importantly, **don't** leave this preparation to the day of the call!

1. Download the software, or application.

2. You may need to create an account to use it. Usually free, it might take a little time to get it working on your computer so get started.

3. If you already have the software on your computer, check for software updates.

4. Check the audio and video settings. If you are not in a private space, do you need headphones and a microphone to cut down background noise?

5. Check your Internet. You need a reliable connection.

6. Are you going to share your screen to show

documents, use 'breakout rooms' or run a video? Get comfortable with how you do that and practise with a colleague or friend.

7. Enable captions: live speech transcription helps people in noisy locations, or those with hearing loss, to more easily follow the discussion.

Host preparations...

Before you do anything, decide:

1. The purpose of the meeting.

2. The desired result.

Then, the detail:

- The date and time

- Who will be invited

- How long the call will be

- What needs to be decided

- Who will take notes

- What happens after the call – the actions required

- What happens if the Internet connection fails and how the call will be restarted

Now create an 'agenda' by using the information above and send this out to the invitees at least three working days before the call. People may need more time if the project is complex and diaries are busy.

On your meeting agenda you need:

1. Title, date and time (Check invitee time zones and make it clear to everyone which one you are using!).

2. Confirm the software to be used, for example, Zoom, and instructions for people to join the meeting, including any passwords, links or codes. Most software platforms give you the option to automatically send out links to invitees but it doesn't hurt to put the link again in the agenda to help people.

3. A list of everyone invited.

4. The purpose of the meeting.

5. The points to be discussed.

6. State who will take notes, or 'minutes'. A record of who said what and what was agreed.

7. Outline what will happen if the Internet connection fails.

8. Confirm what will happen when the meeting ends, e.g., who will send out the notes to assign actions and then follow up with people.

Finally, get online early – as host you should always be first, ready to welcome your invitees.

Invitee preparations...

1. Make sure you know the date and time of the meeting (especially different time zones).

2. Check you know how to join the call. Do you need an account, a link or login?

3. Review the agenda and prepare your part of the conversation, including any documents you might need, and note down any questions you may want to ask.

4. You could be helpful by offering to note down what is discussed and agreed (the minutes) and send them to everyone afterwards. This is a great way to develop trust and show commitment to a project.

Now for the virtual meeting itself. Whether you are organising or attending, here's how to create a professional impression online.

BEFORE YOU BEGIN

DO...

- Choose a quiet room free from pets and other people. If the room is carpeted it will help reduce any echo and make your voice easier to hear.

- Sit in front of a light, plain background. Test out some different locations. Some tools, can create a virtual background but be careful, these can be distracting.

- Make sure the space is bright but avoid strong sunlight.

- Use your laptop or desktop computer, not your phone. This keeps the picture steady and means your hands are free to take notes.

- Increase the light on your face with a directional desk lamp.

- Don't be too close to the camera. Try to have your webcam at your eye level, so that people are not staring up your nose or at the top of your head, and have the upper part of your body in view, so that you can also use hand gestures to vary your communication style.

- Know where your camera is and use it to give other participants full eye contact. This improves trust. An arrow on a sticky note next to your camera lens can serve as a reminder of where to look!

- Wear something appropriate, if only on your top half! Show the same respect for others as you would in a face-to-face meeting.

- If you want to share a document with others on the call, check with the host beforehand because, usually, they will need change their settings to allow this during the meeting.

DURING THE MEETING

If you are the host spend a few minutes welcoming everyone, making introductions and checking in on how everyone is doing at the beginning. This may be a virtual meeting, but we should not lose sight of our need for meaningful human connection.

Tell the group the protocol for when someone wants to speak and how to do that, like putting a hand up or using the emojis or message. Run over what the meeting is about and how long it should last. Let people know what will happen if the connection fails.

Host or invitee, DO...

- Give your full attention to the meeting

- Keep your camera on , but give others the option to turn their cameras off, if needed for accessibility or other reasons.

- It is OK to mute your microphone, just ensure you can switch your microphone back on when you begin to speak

- Contribute whenever you can

- Make your own notes

- Be an 'active listener': move, smile, nod in agreement and shift position from time to time, oherwise, people might think you have lost interest, or your connection has frozen

- Thank everyone for their time and contribution

DON'T...

- Arrive late

- Interrupt or speak over people

- Switch your camera off, unless it's been agreed

- Check your emails or social feeds

- Eat

- Play with a pet

- Tidy your space

- Answer a phone call

- Get up and walk away

Tip

Virtual meeting software detects who to show in the main viewing window by noise level – usually this is when someone speaks. It is called 'active speaker'. It's very clever but beware. It also means that when your microphone is on the software will put you in the main viewing window if you sneeze, cough or make other loud noises!

And finally, when the meeting finishes make sure you END the call and CLOSE the software BEFORE you get up, do or say anything else.

Online meetings can be very productive, flexible, even fun! They have helped open up the world to many, many people. Connecting minds across thousands of miles, allowing creative collaboration and fostering better communication. Nothing, however, can replace getting to know one another face-to-face but, done well, virtual meetings can be a great way to connect and advance your business.

"Share what you know, what you love and what you enjoy.

"The miracle is the more we share, the more we have."

Leonard Nimoy
American actor and director; 'Spock' in Star Trek.

Ideas and actions...

"Don't try to win over the haters; you're not a jackass whisperer."

Brené Brown

American professor and best-selling author known for her work on leadership, shame and vulnerability..

Moving Up

Get noticed and build your audience and sales.

- Remember Me?
- Unforgettable
- Email for Sales
- Get Search Engine Friendly
- Putting AI to Work

Remember Me?
The 'elevator pitch', or how to be remembered in 60 seconds

Whether you're networking with other businesses, out shopping, walking or at the school gates, when someone asks you what you do, what do you say? what do you say? What can encapsulate your business and potential in a moment? How do you make yourself memorable?

Interpersonal connections are important to any new startup business, and an elevator pitch is a useful tool. Named after a short elevator ride, as the measure of how long you may get to engage someone before their attention is claimed elsewhere, they can differ depending on the circumstances. You could be at a social gathering, having a casual conversation or be a delegate at a business event. Whatever the situation there are two key elements:

1. What you say – be clear

2. How you make people feel – be remembered

They are about clarity and confidence. Delivering information with enthusiasm. Beginning with a smile, good eye contact, a breath to slow your speech and a positive manner, their purpose is to get people interested. It can take time and practice for you to be happy with yours but it's always worth the effort.

Good elevator pitches are conversation-starters not sales pitches. Here are a couple of examples to answer that, "What do you do?" question.

Tell them WHAT you do through outcomes that will capture their attention; that may be solving a problem, or making people's lives better

Claire: "I help people feel good and more energised."

Edward: "I help people transform their old, tired kitchens and unloved spaces in their homes."

Tell them HOW you do it

Claire: "I'm a fully qualified yoga teacher, I work with people in their own homes and also hold regular local classes."

Edward: "I'm a carpenter specialising in kitchens. I also design bespoke cabinets and shelving."

Tell them WHY you do it, including your personal values

Claire: "I enjoy helping people feel great and become physically stronger. Yoga brings me happiness and lots of health benefits and I love seeing those results in others."

Edward: "I get great satisfaction from making people's lives easier, in more beautiful, purposeful spaces, using different wood for different things. Sustainability is important to me and I use reclaimed wood where I can."

Now, ASK them a question about their lives (and listen to the answer)

> Claire: "Do you often feel tired out at the end of the week?"

> Edward: "I think everyone has an underused space in their home that could do with some love and attention, what do you think?"

The conversation has started and being enthusiastic about your business and interested in your listener's issues helps build trust, connection and curiosity.

Remember to mention how they can FIND and contact you via your website, on LinkedIn, on Instagram, or even at the school gates most days!

> Claire: "If you are interested, I offer free tasters; there's a poster on the bulletin board."

> Edward: "If I can ever help, just let me know; you can see examples of my work on my website."

Today, we can quickly share numbers via our smart phones but don't forget the humble business card. Around since the 16th century, these helpful, wallet-sized marketing tools are still very useful for all contact, social and web information.

Finally, watch out for the pitfalls too by NOT

- Selling
- Using jargon
- Being negative about yourself ("I'm just a..." or "Oh, you won't be interested, but I...")
- Being negative about others
- Exaggerating
- Ignoring your listener's responses

An elevator pitch is a great tool for confidently engaging potential customers, collaborators, supporters and champions: think about and prepare one for different situations, because starting the conversation in the right way can help you find all the right people.

"We are all here on earth to help others; what on earth the others are here for I don't know."

WH Auden
British-American poet, teacher, playwright and literary critic.

Ideas and actions...

"If you can't explain it to a six year old, you don't understand it yourself."

Albert Einstein

German theoretical physicist, creator of the Theory of Relativity and one of the most influential physicists of all time.

Unforgettable
How to write a great strapline

Straplines are used with the names of organisations to give the reader an instant 'hit' of understanding around the product, service, or values that organisation delivers. Done well, straplines are a great way to get remembered, and that's the point.

We're going to look at exactly what a strapline is, and why a strapline is a key branding tool.

What is a strapline, slogan or tag line?

A strapline, slogan or tag line is a short collection of words that accompanies a business name and logo, which can, if well-known enough, be used on its own. Great straplines find a way to encapsulate the aims, ambitions, values and ethos of a brand.

When we get it right, it can become a highly powerful and emotive brand and marketing tool.

Get it wrong and we can become a laughing stock...

To not have one at all is to miss out on a useful branding opportunity!

Dating back to the advent of mass manufacturing in the late 1800s, straplines are as popular as ever. Here are some highly successful straplines:

Think Different	Apple
Just Do It	Nike
Because you're worth it	L'Oreal
Reassuringly expensive	Stella Artois
Does exactly what it says on the tin	Ronseal
Feel every word	Waterstones
Liquid engineering	Castrol GTX engine oil

When we read these, we'll know many, if not all of them. And, they all have one thing in common. None of them mention either the business name or the products they produce. That's because it is not the job of the strapline to tell you the business name or the product.

The job of a strapline is to appeal to our emotions.

Straplines reflect our desires; promote positive action; offer glamour; lifestyle ambition; reassurance; security and even excitement.

These brands know their markets and their customers, and they are appealing directly to them. The straplines define, in a few words the essence of the product and its relationship to a consumer. And because they are short and appealing, we remember them.

Humour can also play a role in straplines in crowded market places, how about this strapline?

"We're the last ones to let you down..."
- local undertakers

What is a bad strapline?

Overly wordy and confusing. How about this, printed on a flyer I received from a large office supplies company, let's call it Stylus.

"What you do today improves all your tomorrows"

Really? Does it? For me, this strapline says nothing with too many words. I mean, you might do something today that ruins tomorrow and that may include buying something from Stylus. It's not specific or ambitious enough – we can do better than 'improves' surely? It is bland. It has no power, no emotion.

A better strapline might be: **"Stick it!"**

This encapsulates getting the job done. Working hard for a good outcome. Completing the task. Landing the jump. It has force and suggests resilience and all those colourful little sticky pads that I love! It also has alliteration in the use of the 'S' of 'Stylus' and 'Stick'.

It could also be a good strapline for glue for lots of the same reasons!

It can also be a rude way to tell people to push off.

You see how tricky straplines it can be?

But, which strapline would you remember?

Bad straplines also escape into the world when a business confuses its mission statement with its strapline.

A mission statement tells people the purpose, aims and values of the business.

> Stylus – We aim to produce and sell the best quality, the widest range and most affordable office supplies anywhere.

A strapline tells people why they should buy from that business.

> Stylus – Stick it!

When it comes to working out a good strapline for your business there's a short six-point plan to help us come up with the right combination of words and, importantly, make it memorable.

1. Keep it simple (six words maximum and alliteration can help brains remember phrases

2. Make it meaningful

3. Be honest

4. Give the benefits

5. Be original

6. Project personality

Look around for other straplines that appeal to you. Think about why that is? Are you their target market? Are they funny? Weird? Inspiring? Why do they work?

It can be a quite a process to find the one that's right for you and it may well change over time as your business evolves. At each part of the process sit and live with it for a while, get feedback from a range of colleagues and associates until you find something that really speaks for and about your business.

Finally, you never know 100% what's going to work. I always think of German car manufacturer Audi's famous strapline from the 1980s, created by a British advertising copywriter whose visit to the factory meant he spotted an old slogan on a faded poster.

Vorsprung durch Technik

Translated as "progress through technology", not many people in Britain understood it, and it doesn't really say anything, but its appeal was such that it has become part of British culture for describing technical excellence and resilience. This brings us neatly on to translating straplines for different countries.

"When a slogan is translated, we must think long and hard both about what's important to us and about what's important to our readers. We also need to consider what our readers already know, so that we don't say things that don't need to be said.

In short:

Context is king

"Our own understanding of words and phrases and that of our readers. The unstated knowledge that both sides of the content equation – creator and reader – share in one way or another.

"It's a big part of why machine translation (Google Translate, for example) can go so laughably wrong. A computer algorithm simply can't understand the unstated knowledge or context, or subtext of any given sentence. It can't know why a writer chose a certain word or what exactly a reader will understand or, more importantly, feel when that word is used."

Grey Drane
Copywriter and translator.

Here's a great example of why using local knowledge and native translators is so important. Pepsi upset its Chinese consumers when it didn't realise its "Come alive with Pepsi" slogan directly translated as "Pepsi brings your ancestors back from the dead."

Or how about: McDonald's Big Mac in France, directly translated as "Gros Mec," which actually means, "big pimp."

Or even more delightful: Frank Perdue's Chicken's strapline

for Spanish markets went from "It takes a strong man to make a tender chicken" to "It takes an aroused man to make a chicken affectionate."*

Not great. But very funny.

*With thanks to www.businessinsider.com for those nuggets.

"Always remember: a brand is the most valuable piece of real estate in the world; a corner of someone's mind."

John Hegarty
Author and leading UK advertising creative.

Ideas and actions...

"Most people never ask. That's what separates the people that do things from those who just dream about them."

Steve Jobs
Visionary and pioneer of personal computing – co-founder of Apple, he was involved in creating the iPod, and iPhone. He also founded Pixar Animation Studios.

Emails for Sales
How to get results from email marketing

We are all used to emails. In our working and home lives many of us will have different email addresses for personal and professional correspondence, as we navigate the seemingly unending flow of information that lands every day. With so much email traffic and the undesirable proliferation of 'spam' and online scams, are emails still a good way to sell goods and services? Well, yes, they are and, as with all successful marketing, it comes down to research and planning.

Many emails don't get opened. We browse down the list of the new arrivals and immediately bin those we don't like the look of. Email software is also getting better at filtering out spam and potential threats into our 'junk' folders, so we need to have a clear plan and a transparent approach to avoid the junk folder and engage our customers' attention.

Delivered directly to people's inboxes, emails can:

- Be highly targeted to capture attention

- Engage and build trust

- Remind customers of your worth

- Make customers feel valued

- Deliver useful information

In order to generate sales from emails we need to use a consistent approach that will give us the best opportunity of engagement. This means the creation of four important elements.

1. **Selection** – decide who you want to receive your email.

2. **Subject text** – a good reason to open your email.

3. **Sell** – like all good stories you need:

    i.   A beginning

    ii. A middle

    iii. An end

    iv. A call to action

    v.   A sign-off

4. **Strategy** – decide on your follow-up plan and how it fits within your wider marketing mix.

In this guide we're going to look at ensuring you have all the elements to launch a successful email sales campaign that will bring you results.

1. Selection – who is going to receive the email?

For an email campaign you need people's emails. And, not just anyone's. You want the emails of people who you believe will be interested in what you're selling. So start gathering…

Whenever you engage with a potential customer, or

someone who is just interested in what you are doing, you need to gather their basic contact details (with their permission) and begin building your database. This database should be growing right from the moment you decide to go into business, but it's never too late to begin!

In its simplest form, your database may be a spreadsheet of names and details, for example in a Microsoft Excel or a Google Sheets document. This will keep all your contacts in one place but that's all it will do. The best thing to do is take advantage of a free email management tool.

Email management software like, Mailchimp and HubSpot, offer free versions to help you manage your mailing lists, create campaigns and design professional, imaginative emails. You can also segment your contacts based on their last purchase, interest, location or any number of different ways.

You will also be able to see who has opened your email, clicked on your links and more. This information is important to understanding what your contacts are truly interested in. It will also give you the ability to test and measure your subject lines, sales copy and images on different groups of customers to find out what gives better results. There are plenty more email management tools available, so do some research and see which one will suit you.

Be sure to read the section at the end of this chapter on email marketing and the law.

2. Subject – first thing's first, or is it?

The subject line is critical to get right: it's how you'll encourage people to OPEN your email. The process of writing your email can often give you the best idea for the subject line, so don't worry about the subject now – we're going to come back to it later!

3 – Sell: how will we convince someone to buy from us in a short email?

When I go shopping without a list I always end up buying things I never wanted and not buying the things I need. So to avoid wasting time and effort, we need a list: a step by step approach to creating a great email that we can replicate. Let's start with what we know:

1. Our customer wants a solution to a problem (maybe one they didn't even know they had).

2. We have the answer.

Key to any marketing is understanding our customers, our 'target market'; understanding the problem, need or aspiration of our customers. Knowing this means we can get their attention and offer them the solution.

Tone and language. The tone needs to be friendly, confident, personal, professional. Make them feel like they matter, because they do!

i. A beginning

Dear Ted /   Good afternoon Sarah / Hello Dr Brown / Hi Ben!

> 71% of customers say they are more likely to open a personalised email from a brand or company.
> *Dynamic Yield Research*

How we address our customers depends on our market research and the kind of customers we want to attract. Keep in mind IT'S ALL ABOUT THEM. "Hey there", "Hello" or "Good morning" isn't good enough. If you know their names, use them respectfully.

Now ... get to the point (remember people are busy).

In two sentences tell them WHY you are getting in touch. This helps build trust and helps to keep them reading.

For example: I hope you are well. I'm getting in touch because I...

- Have a new 'how to guide' to share

- Have a seasonal discount offer on my...

- A new product coming soon

- Am in the area

- Have availability for late bookings

- Would welcome an opportunity to talk to you about...

In the next sentence, tell them WHAT you are offering and HOW it will benefit them ...

For example I wanted to let you know, so that you.

- Can get more from [a particular product/service/interest]

- Don't miss out on new lines and discounted stock

- Get 'early bird' offers

- Don't have to travel to meet me

- Can still book me, flexible and hassle free!

- Can receive a free, no-obligation quote...

Having told them WHY you are getting in touch and WHAT'S in it for them, they are now going to want reassurance.

ii. A middle

This section is about reassuring your email reader about your trustworthiness and expertise.

In a few sentences talk about the people or businesses you have already helped. Give evidence of results, include a testimonial from another customer (don't make these up and do link them to the testimonial on your website). Remind your reader of the problem you're solving for them and the benefits your customer can relate to. Use bullet points as this helps a reader who is quickly scanning the screen. For example:

Trained in Paris, where I worked with several of Europe's top design houses, including Chanel and Dior. I have helped hundreds of people like you feel great and look fantastic in a hat, all at affordable prices.

"My hat was the perfect finishing touch. I had so many compliments, it made me feel and look a million dollars. Wide choice and fast delivery made it a great experience." Alexis

- Weddings

- Special occasions

- Race days

- Any day!

Buy or hire – a short, no-obligation consultation is all it takes and I have availability in person or online.

If what you sell is highly visual – such as clothing, jewellery and home products – one stunning picture is worth a thousand words. BUT be careful – the image needs to be optimised for email traffic and some people's email providers will block images. This is another reason to look at an email management tool because they can allow you to use a professional design with plenty of images.

iii. An end

Tell your potential customer how much you would like to help THEM. It can be another way to show them you understand their problem, for example:

> The affordable way to look a million dollars: I'd love to help you to look great and feel fabulous in a hat. I offer a bespoke design service, or why not check out my hire collection? Let's start planning your perfect look today.

iv. A call to action (CTA)

Importantly, after persuading your readers what you sell is perfect for them, TELL THEM WHAT TO DO.

Give them a link to your website where they can browse more products and buy. Or offer them a phone number to call, a response form, sign up to a newsletter to create more regular engagement. For example:

Click here to buy now and get 15% OFF your designer hat with code SUPERHAT15.

or

Click here to book a no-obligation appointment today and get 10% off hire or purchase.

or

Sign up to my newsletter here for fresh trends, top tips, seasonal discounts and more...

or

Visit my website for seasonal ideas, the latest looks and monthly discount codes.

Adding a discount code will help you track who's responding to your email. You can also create a sense of urgency by making any offer or discount time sensitive, for example:

- Don't miss out! Your discount code is only valid for the next 24 hours.

- Only 5 left and going fast!

- Due to demand this offer expires at the end of [date]

- Take advantage of our 'early bird' price, ends [date]

There is also another little trick to keep your audience engaged and capture their details. Giving people who are not sure a reason to stay in touch. For example:

Now not the right time? Sign up to my monthly newsletter and get 10% OFF for the next six months with my thanks for staying in touch. Including exclusive offers and seasonal trends, don't worry, you are free to unsubscribe at any time.

v. A sign-off

A signature or 'sign-off', gives us another opportunity to reinforce our message and sell by providing links to our website, blogs, podcasts, image gallery and social feeds, such as Instagram and Facebook.

Another tip

Use a P.S. line in your email signature to link to a relevant case study, blog, work sample or product line that would further interest people in your business. Connect to your other marketing tools to give choice and more reasons to take you seriously.

For example:

> Best wishes,
>
> Cherry B
>
> Get ahead, get a hat
>
> Visit my gallery for inspiration and the latest trends.
>
> Follow me on <u>Instagram</u> and <u>Facebook</u> for my latest offers and discount codes.
>
> P.S. Did you know that for a fraction of the cost to buy, you can hire a sensational special occasion hat? Read my latest blog _Turning Heads on a Tiny Budget._

Finally, remember our subject line?

Having written the main part of your email it is often now easier to write a great subject line because you've done the hard work of deciding exactly what needs to be said and how. Here's what to think about …

Don't make it misleading – once people find out that the email is not what they were led to believe, you'll never get them back. It does more harm than good.

Be human. This may be a sales email but remember you're talking to people; think about how you're helping them and solving their problems. Make it relatable to them.

Tip

Start the subject line with a capital letter but leave the rest lower case. It has a 'softer' more human appeal and less the title of a lecture!

If you decide to make the subject a question, be very sure you give the answer when they open the email, otherwise it is frustrating for them.

Sticking with the example of our hat seller, a good subject line would be:

How to turn heads on a tiny budget

Tip
Emojis can make subject lines appealing to the eye, but don't over use them, be professional.

Tip

Try to avoid exclamation marks and use of all capitals, it can feel like you're SHOUTING!

So, we have an outline of how to put together a great sales email with all the information, reassurance and contact details. Finally, don't make the email too long: people don't have time to read an essay and, remember, the most important part is the benefits to your customer and getting them to take action by visiting a website, signing up to a newsletter or getting in direct contact.

4. Strategy

Sales emails can be an effective part of your marketing mix. It can take up to seven 'touches' of contact before someone will commit to buying something. A 'touch' may be seeing your post on social media, a poster in a shop or advert in a magazine, seeing your website when browsing, being recommended by a friend AS WELL AS reading your sales email. It takes time to build trust and encourage people to buy from you and you will need to be consistent with timing and quality.

Being where your customers are shopping is the key along with consistent, regular contact. When you send out your emails, be that weekdays, weekends, morning or evening, will depend on your customers' shopping habits, but remember to change it up, so that they see emails at different times.

The follow-up plan

After the first sales email goes out, your work has only just begun...

Your plan and timescale for following up will depend on your market and what you are offering, but as an example:

1. Send a thank you email to everyone who responds, regardless of any action they take.

2. For those who do respond, follow up quickly by doing what was promised. Note what they bought and when – to inform the next email to them – they are now 'loyal customers'.

3. For people who don't respond,

    •   After a week, create and send out a shorter, reminder email, summing up your first email and reiterating any time-sensitive offers.

- After a month, create a follow-up email with a fresh approach, but similar content.

- Monitor the results. What worked, what didn't? Adjust what you do and prepare the next sales email campaign. This time your contacts will be divided into a. new business, and b. previous responders and current customers.

a. new business
b. for responders and current customers

Remember to try different subject lines with different segments, discover what's more popular and use that knowledge to attract more people.

If you are selling fashion items and your stock changes quickly, you will want to send more frequent emails. If you are an architect, your approach is likely to be different instead of regularly changing goods you may choose to offer a monthly newsletter on architecture and design to keep your customers and contacts interested and engaged. Again, it comes back to how your customers make their buying decisions.

Email marketing can be a numbers game: the more people we reach the better chance we have of getting results. Targeting our emails to the right people, however, will always increase our chances of success.

Finally, don't get stuck in your ways. People's attention and desires change. Experiment with the format and images, test and measure to keep sales emails fresh and producing worthwhile results.

Read our guide on getting the right marketing mix to see how sales emails can work alongside your other areas of marketing such as websites, social media and newsletters.

Email marketing and the law

When we use people's emails for marketing purposes, it's important to know and abide by the law relating to people's privacy rights. For example, in the UK and Europe it is the General Data Protection Regulation (GDPR) which sets out how we can legally collect and use people's personal information for marketing purposes. Misuse is a criminal offence. Make sure to check your country's law on email marketing standards and abide by it.

Ideas and actions...

Choose to care, preserve and protect.
It's an attractive quality.

"Nobody cares how much you know, until they know how much you care."

Theodore Roosevelt
Soldier, conversationalist, naturalist, historian, writer and President of the United States from 1901 to 1909.

Get Search Engine Friendly
A startup guide to search engine optimisation

Search engines like Google and Bing use very sophisticated algorithms within their web crawler software to determine which websites they list and in what order. These algorithms also evolve as search engines to adapt and improve what they do. Search engine optimisation (SEO) describes techniques by which we can refine the content of our websites to help the web crawlers – also called bots or spiders – to find, index and list our websites.

Nearly 30%* of people searching for stuff online will click on the first organic (unpaid for) result delivered on Google's top page.

As a startup, with small budgets and big ambitions, this tells us two important things:

1. People don't just click on the top results, which are usually 'pay per click' adverts.

2. In order to get listed as near to the top as possible on the search engine results pages (SERPs), it's important to use SEO techniques on our websites.

* 2022 CTR Survey by Banklinko.

In this guide we're going to look at how to apply basic SEO techniques to website pages. Our focus is SEO for content – the metadata, or text, that we can place on our website to help the web crawlers locate, index and rank it. Website visitors don't see metadata, it's there to help the search engines, so it's worth taking advantage of the opportunity!

At this point it's worth underlining that a good search engine optimised website is the product of several things, most importantly:

1. The website is well built using current best practice covering design, typography and functionality.

2. The content should be high quality and unique (not copied from someone else).

3. The website is reactive for use on PC as well as tablet and mobile phone.

4. Images and videos are of high quality.

5. It is accessible to those with visual impairments.

Along with metadata, these elements all play a role in how well a website will rank on results pages. Cutting corners in the basics will mean poor search engine results in the long run.

If we don't choose to input our own crafted metadata on to our websites, search engine bots will choose it for us, and this can vary from OK to not great at all. So let's give them all the help they need.

The world is searching ... back to the metadata

A search term, or query, is the word, phrase or question typed into the search box of a search engine to find information. It might be a single word, a phrase, or a question. The more specific the search term the better and Google loves you to ask questions, so that it can find relevant and appropriate answers to help you.

If we simply type the search term "Micro Oiseau" into the search box and click 'enter' or 'return' on our keyboard, at time of writing this, the following appears:

---

https://www.micro-oiseau.com

Micro Oiseau • marketing for micro entrepreneurs and startups

Micro Oiseau: marketing guides & resources for startups. 'How to Be in Business' mindset & marketing book. Business templates | translation.

Here's what is returned when we type "Nike"

---

https://www.nike.com

Nike. Just Do It. Nike UK

Any Place. Any Time. Any Condition. Be Your Best Every Time With **Nike** Shoes And Clothing.

You can see that these organic listings acts like mini adverts for a website, a simple organic listing will include:

website address
SEO title
SEO description or excerpt of text
Any search word or phrase shown in bold

Let's say we are a micro entrepreneur startup and we make fantastic hats and live in York. Naturally, we want our website to feature high on the SERPs so people can find us when they need a hat. They may live in York, or they could live anywhere in the world.

Most people won't have heard of us so won't know to search our business name to find us online. In this case we need to help search engines rank our website for information about hat design and making in York. People like to use questions to search, rather than just type words into the search box, and we need to bear this in mind when we produce content for our website. We need to think about:

1. Who are our **readers?**

2. What is our main **message?**

3. What do we want people to **learn?**

This insight helps us decide on the focus of our content; what key words, phrases and questions we need to use and answer, and want our web page to be found for.

Do your research. Ask people, colleagues and friends, and look at competitor websites.

There are free tools to help you research key words, including Ubersuggest, Google Trends, Ahrefs Keyword Generator and WordStream, amongst many others. There are also chatbots, or AI language processing tools, that can help identify the questions most searched for on a topic. They do this by mining the Internet for subject-specific searches and this can be another handy way to work out what key words to use on your website. Have a look at Microsoft-developed ChatGPT, Google's Bard and Jasper. Not always free, take advantage of a free trial period.

Our key words will need to be included within page titles, headings and page text in as natural way as possible.

Be wary of using these chatbots to write your content for you! They are taking content that already exists and repackaging it – you could end up using someone else's words or repeating flawed, inaccurate content. It is always best to write your own unique content.

The instructions around inputting metadata sit in the code of the webpages themselves. Few of us are coders capable of building our own websites, so pre-built website templates are a great way to begin.

If you are using a pre-built website template from a company such as WordPress, take advantage of free software like Yoast. It offers a way to add SEO information in a simple format. Other website providers like Squarespace or Wix, among others, also give options to add SEO text easily, along with 'how to' guides to set up your SEO correctly. Check the web software you are using. If you are having your website built from scratch, ask your developer to include the ability for you to add SEO metadata and text easily.

Be aware: when using a pre-built website template you may be offered a way to set up the SEO text across multiple pages at once. This means a fast and easy set up, but the most effective SEO comes from crafting unique meta text for each individual page to reflect the content and images more closely.

Here's what to know

Let's say our website name is www.happyhats.com and our key words for a particular page includes 'hat makers' because the page is going to be all about the staff.

We need to use our key words in...

Page Title: Our hat makers

The page title will be included in the URL for the page, as follows:

www.happyhats.com/our-hat-makers

Content: place your text within the design template in the appropriate sections. Try to use your key term(s) in the first paragraph, as part of your headings and in the body of the text. But remember, don't be tempted to use your key terms too often, your text should always read naturally. The sophistication of web crawler software means they will downgrade a website that uses what's called 'key word stuffing'.

The length of your text is also important. Google likes us to use around 300 words +.

Good quality images: added from your website image library. Take care to use the key terms as part of the image 'alt text description' as this is picked up by web crawlers.

Metadata or 'tags'

SEO Title or Meta Title: not the same as the page title, the meta title forms the page navigation tab for search engine browsers and is important. Remember our example of an organic listing? The meta title appears in large type below the URL or website address. Use your key term first and include the name of your site and more if you can. Keep it to 50–60 characters, including spaces, and use separators to help readers.

Meta Description: approach these like mini adverts for the content of the page and make sure to use key terms. The recommended length is 50 to 160 characters, including spaces.

> **When it comes to hat makers, we have a very talented team! For the best hats in York, visit our workshop and meet us.**

For our example, when someone types the question, "Are there hat makers in York?" into the search engine query box, here's what our organic listing will look like:

www.happyhats.com/our-hat-makers

Hat Makers | Happy Hats York | get ahead, get a hat

Meet our **hat makers**! Proud of our talented team, for the best hats in **York**, visit our workshop and come and meet us.

Note that the search engine has picked out the question search terms in bold. Location is important for local queries.

Add a 'feature image' for the page. You may get an option to add a feature image and these may appear in the listings next to the description text. They make the search results look much richer and more appealing so why not use them? Don't forget to fill in the alt text section for the image!

... and there's more!

Links

Search engines like content that is relevant and connected.

Internal links from one web page to another within websites also help SEO. So, try to include internal links to other, relevant pages that also support visitor experience; an, 'if you like this, you may like this' approach.

Outbound links

Search engines also like us to link out to other websites that are relevant to ours. When creating these outbound links, it is important to ensure that they open in a new browser window so that our visitors can return to our site.

This is done in the link options when you create the link, so remember to check!

Backlinks

These are links to our sites from other websites. They must be relevant and high quality. In other words they should be well-built, relevant websites; any old website backlink won't do, in fact it may harm our ranking. It's a good idea to ask associates, suppliers and partners to include a link to your site using your business name and do the same for them. It will help their SEO too!

By following these basic steps you can search optimise your website and give yourself the best chance of attracting the attention of the search engines. When a new website goes live it can take a few months for it to be indexed and start to rank. When you consider that millions of websites go live every day that's possibly not surprising. It can be a waiting game.

The next step, once your website is ranking, is to keep updating your content with fresh text and images. It is also worth refining your SEO metadata as your content changes.

Test and measure

Google Analytics is powerful suite of free tools that can tell you the traffic, or visits, your website is attracting; how people are finding you; what devices they are using; where in the world they are; what key words people are using to find you and lots more. All this will further help you improve your SEO. To find out how to access Google Analytics you need to have a Google account email address and password, then register for Google Analytics. After registering follow the online instructions to access your website information.

Paying for digital adverts – pay-per-click

The search engines offer ways for you to beat the ranking by paying to have your listings placed at the top or the bottom of leading pages. It works with key words and you only pay a fee when someone clicks on your listing. The amount you pay, however, depends on your sector. Highly competitive sectors like hospitality and retail mean high prices and you'll be paying a lot to get a few clicks.

If you want to get visitors quickly then pay-per-click (PPC) may work in the short term, depending on your budget.

If you want to grow with a steady build of visitor traffic, post high quality content consistently, underpinned with a sound SEO strategy. It is better and cheaper than PPC in the long run.

Many businesses choose to use both techniques, with PPC used for specific campaigns. For more on using PPC simply ask your nearest search engine!

Ideas and actions...

Recognise that the time to rest and recharge is just as important as the time to push towards your goals.

"Nothing in nature blooms all year round. And neither will you."

Anon

Putting AI to Work

Chatbots for business – the good, the bad and the ugly; what you need to know about natural language artificial intelligence and how to use it

Artificial intelligence (AI) describes human processes done by machines, largely computer programming that can do tasks traditionally only humans could, such as processing data, recognising patterns, learning and making decisions. In effect, a simulation of human intelligence. A natural language AI or 'chatbot' allows computer programmes to respond directly to input from a human in a conversational format. Apple's Siri and Amazon's Alexa are voice-activated natural language AI systems. Designed by the company OpenAI, I asked the chatbot ChatGPT, "What do you do?" Here's its response:

> "As an AI chatbot, I am designed to simulate conversation with human users through text or voice interactions. I use natural language processing and machine learning algorithms to understand and respond to user input in a way that is informative.

* My wonderful illustrator Ned Hoste took one of his cartoons and briefed AI to create a similar one in the style of Leonardo da Vinci!

"I can provide information on a wide range of topics by performing web searches and presenting the results in a concise and easy-to-understand manner. I can also generate creative content such as poems, stories, and songs, and help users with rewriting, improving, or optimising their own content.

"I am constantly learning from my interactions with users and updating my knowledge base to provide more accurate and relevant responses. However, my actions are limited to responding to user input within the chat box, and my internal knowledge is only current up until a certain point in time.

"Overall, my goal is to provide users with a positive and engaging experience by providing helpful information and assistance in a friendly and respectful manner."

So there you have it! AI is a way to find out things, write, edit and produce content, as well as research subjects. But along with the many benefits of this technology, there are warnings as well.

There are both benefits and risks to using AI in business.

The business benefits of AI

AI can help save you time and boost your productivity. By automating and optimising repetitive, day-to-day tasks, it can free up space for you to take on more interesting and creative ones. It can cut down the time taken to analyse data, research your market, draft content and automate certain aspects of customer service.

Four popular ways to use chatbots are to:

1. **Answer questions.** By typing in your question and giving the question some parameters and context, the chatbot will generate a response based on its knowledge and understanding of the topic.

2. **Generate content.** It can be used to help generate and edit content such as blogs and social media posts, stories poems, and songs.

3. **Support search engine optimisation ...SEO.** It can help research top key words and help write meta text to optimise online content.

4. **Debug code.** It can be used to help debug code by asking clarifying questions and providing suggestions for fixing errors.

5. **Research.** It can be used as a research tool, providing detailed responses to questions on a wide range of topics.

Using AI chatbots to support customers' frequently asked questions is already popular, freeing up time and resources for a business to focus on helping other customers with more complex needs. Increasingly sophisticated in replicating the language and tone of human responders, they are, however, still relatively easy to spot and can lead to customer frustration. And that's not all that can be frustrating about this new business tool.

The business risks of AI

There are potential risks associated with using AI in business. Remember, this 'intelligence' is mining the Internet for its information and, although it is continually learning, it can only learn from already published material, some of which is biased and incorrect. Relying on flawed information leads to poor decision making and unfair outcomes, reputational damage and loss of trust.

Remember, ChatGPT itself warns us:

> "... my actions are limited to responding to user input within the chat box, and my internal knowledge is only current up until a certain point in time."

The quality of AI's response is also only as good as the quality and detail of the questions we ask it. You may find you need to ask your question in a number of different ways before you make progress.

AI doesn't know your business or your customer and you'll need to edit any response you get for the right language and tone of voice.

AI is not always right! Used for data research, query terms and knowledge 'lag' will impact AI's response, together with its understanding of the topic, which may not be broad and certainly won't be not hands-on! More on this later...

Despite this, AI is already a powerful tool, for example, in medical science AI is supporting doctors in diagnostics and surgery. Quickly assimilating information from vast databases, combined with robotic technology, it can perform tasks requiring pinpoint accuracy repeatedly with consistent effort and no errors without getting tired or being distracted. That is something that humans, with our complex brains, lives and personalities find hard, if not impossible, to do.

But, tethered to exisiting information, AI can't make a leap of faith, dream or make seemingly unconnected links to create world-changing disruptive products and processes. AI does not have an inspired or unique approach to complex problems. Whilst, with the ability to create and sustain relationships through empathy and an emotional response, humans are experts at:

Awareness

Creativity

Curiosity

Emotion

Empathy

Grasping the subtleties of cultural contexts and emotional responses is beyond AI.

This lack of humanity is especially evident in translation, where AI regularly fails, incapable of conveying the correct meaning of words that are bound up in the historic and cultural experience of a community, ethnic group or nation.

Relationships are built on us listening to our customers, just as much, if not more than simply responding to them.

AI listens to respond.

Humans listen to understand.

And understanding builds TRUST. Without trust there is no business.

Firing up the imagination

Humans can be, at times, chaotic and random. We rely on 'gut instinct', experience and assessing another human being's body language and tone of voice. We are also expert storytellers with the ability to weave a story, to captivate and engage, firing up another's imagination. Two people will never tell the same story in the same way, even witnessing an event together at first hand. It is the beauty and the burden of being human that we have this capacity for such individual responses, driven by our own unique perspective and experience of life.

"Building the new ..." the best use of AI for business

Widely credited as the founder of Western philosophy, Socrates lived nearly two and a half thousand years ago in Athens and then, just like today, people were challenged by the 'new'.

"The secret of change is to focus all your energy, not on fighting the old, but on building the new."

Socrates

Whilst technology has evolved, human nature has not. Wary of change, we are all challenged by the 'new', it's a protection mechanism. However, we also need to heed Socrates's advice and continue to adapt to succeed.

Putting AI to work

With an understanding of the benefits and challenges of AI, what's the best way to make AI work for us?

In the early, pioneering days of computer science, a US Army mathematician William D Mellin coined the phrase, "Garbage in, garbage out" to describe how computers can't think for themselves and that a computer's output can only be as useful and accurate as the quality of the data that's input.

In 2023 this was confirmed by New Zealand supermarket Pak 'n' Save's AI meal planner app called Savey Meal-bot. The app was developed to help customers navigate the high cost of living and reduce their weekly bills by using up leftover food.

By inputting various ingredients the app would auto generate a meal recipe with a jaunty text commentary. Things went wrong, however, when customers started inputting non-food items. One auto generated recipe entitled Aromatic Water Mix, was proudly described as, "the perfect non-alcoholic beverage to quench your thirst and refresh your senses", yet this delightfully sounding drink actually created chlorine gas, and while the app went on to encourage users to "serve chilled and enjoy the refreshing fragrance", it also went on to warn that inhaling chlorine gas can cause lung damage or death. Not a great start to any cocktail party.

Gleefully, it appears app users went on to explore what other 'recipes' the app could create and the results included "glue sandwiches" and "bleach-infused rice surprise". Deeply disgruntled supermarket execs were embarrassed and disappointed by its misuse. Vowing to keep refining the tool, a warning notice has since been added to the instructions informing users that, "recipes are not reviewed by a human being" and there are no guarantees that any recipe will be "suitable for consumption".

The input, questions or 'prompts' we use are the key to exploiting AI to our benefit. It's the difference between useful and useless.

Creating great AI prompts

Thoughtful, well-crafted prompts mean higher quality responses so think of AI is as your junior, by that I mean a human assistant: less experienced in the sector, keen but a bit prone to go off on a tangent and not too careful where they get their information from in their enthusiasm to please you.

This junior team member is going to do better when you provide them with as much background, context and specifics as possible to help ensure they find what you need in the shortest time, and that could include:

Researching

Exploring your potential audience, your 'ideal customer', sector, market and competitors. Learn about a particular sector by looking at customer frustration, pain points, FAQs, needs and seasonal buying habits.

Editing and simplifying

Exploring different tones of voice, formal and informal presentation of text; reducing word count for social media posts or articles; simplifying complex concepts; proofreading and swapping out jargon for plain English.

Content inspiration

Explore different ideas for content creation with a particular market in mind; discover what matters to your audience and what messages will resonate with them. Educate yourself with what competitors, influencers and experts are doing and saying.

Search engine optimisation

Identify key words for your market to support your website copy and SEO, organising them into users' search intent: informational, navigational and transactional; create meta descriptions and titles for your pages.

Top tips for AI prompts

1. Write as if you are instructing an inexperienced member of the team; include plenty of background detail, descriptions and context, be clear on the outcome you want to reach.

   Here's a simple example for two different prompts for the same business; think about your own business, which is going to give richer, more useful results?

   Prompt 1: What key words should a housebuilder use on their website?

   Prompt 2: I am a housebuilder based in Southampton, UK. I've been building houses for over 30 years and am very experienced. Working with my son and daughter I build luxury homes with eco fittings like solar panels and air source heat pumps. I use heritage and contemporary designs and create beautiful gardens. I want to emphasise the bespoke nature of my work and that I can also help with planning applications. What key words should I use on my website?

   When you get the first answer back, don't settle, dig deeper. Ask more specific questions with more detailed background to increase the AI tool's understanding of what you want to learn.

2. Context is very important to help AI focus its responses to your needs. Put yourself in your customers' shoes when looking for information, ideas and inspiration for your marketing; think of it like briefing a marketing agency. For example, if you run a yoga studio and you want to attract more young men, ask AI to assume an identify and/or a profession before asking your questions.

   Prompt: I'm a 22-year-old man and I am putting on too much weight because I have desk job in the middle of the city. I want to go to an exercise class but am nervous. What messages would help convince me to get motivated and try an early morning yoga class?

3. Help your decision making process by asking for 'pros' and 'cons' around a subject. Just remember your prompt needs to be accompanied by plenty of context and background to support your individual situation or the response will be too general.

4. When creating content use AI for ideas and inspiration. Don't simply cut and paste what it gives you. By and large this will be too generic and you should want to make it more bespoke to you and your business. Use the AI version as a draft that you can work on and improve with personal anecdotes and your unique perspective. Again, work with it like a junior assistant. Ask for more detail, or a better quote or shift the tone of voice and word count. It's important to avoid using anyone else's work that the AI tool may give you. This would be plagiarism. Use a plagiarism checker to avoid this. Check out Copyscape, Grammarly or Quetext.

5. Importantly, when researching always ask AI to cite its sources. This will help keep it honest and give you more insight and additional research links for relevant, trustworthy and useful information.

What you ask your AI chatbot is limited only by your own experience, understanding and ambition. Whatever you need, ensuring that you write high-quality prompts will undoubtedly give you the best chance of exploiting AI's mighty reach.

Supporting you with data, research and content drafts; an unpaid, on-call 24-hour assistant, let AI do its job gathering information, organising data and streamlining mundane tasks, saving time and money through its indefatigable work rate, while you get on with yours: staying connected, engaged and creative; taking advantage of new opportunities and supporting others with an appealing, engaging and profitable business.

I have discussed ChatGPT built by OpenAI, but there are many more AI tools available with different skill sets, such as image and music creation. These tools will only improve, so there's no time like the present to get curious and use AI to your advantage.

Ideas and actions...

More Help

Handy guides to give you the edge
Delivering, Locating, Navigating
Free Image Library

"Eighty percent of success is showing up."

Woody Allen

Actor and multi-award-winning screenwriter.

Delivering, Locating, Navigating

Knowing the right three little words means you'll always know where you're going

The team behind what3words has given a unique combination of three words to every single three-metre square on earth.

When you know those words you can find someone or something with amazing accuracy.

The words are chosen at random but never change.

Join thousands of entrepreneurs and businesses all around the world using what3words to:

 be found

 find others

 save lives

With the what3words app, it's easy to find, share and save precise locations.

Visit the website and find out how what3words can support your business. https://what3words.com/business

Ideas and actions...

We are more creative when we are having fun: more curious and more innovative.

"What makes you different, or weird, that's your strength."

Meryl Streep
Academy Award Winning American actress

Free Image Library
Choose from thousands of great free images, cartoons and photography

Great for illustrating social media, blogs, websites, digital and print marketing projects and campaigns, here's our list of good online stock libraries:

- unsplash.com
- pixabay.com
- pexels.com
- stocksnap.io
- lifeofpix.com
- freepik.com
- freerangestock.com
- picjumbo.com
- gratisography.com
- pikwizard.com

The above websites offer free imagery and also images you will be charged for. So double check what you are choosing and read the terms and conditions of use.

Tip

For websites and social media download png and jpeg file formats.

Flickr

Flickr.com is a worldwide website for sharing photography. A free account will allow you to search thousands of images. There are plenty of images that are available for public use under a Creative Commons license, whereby you may use the image as long as you credit the creator. You will find all the information on the different licenses on Flickr's license page.

For free Illustration, cartoons and graphics for advertising and social media, check out **undraw.co**.

BE WISE, watch out for the © and stay away from **Google Images**. '© All Rights Reserved' means the image is protected and you cannot use it without permission from the owner or creator. Whatever image library you use, be wise and always check the Use license. If an image displays a watermark or copyright symbol © on the image, or in accompanying information, it means it is protected and you may not use it without permission or paying a license fee. Just because an image is on Google Images DOES NOT mean you can use it for your business.

Free design tools

A useful image creation tool, **canva.com** helps you create website graphics and social media header images for all the popular social media platforms. Starter accounts are free and give you a choice of free template designs or you can upload your own images and text to create your own unique design. Again, a fee-based version offers greater design help and functionality.

Keep your image files small and your website fast

Many photographic images will be very large files. This means they will be good quality, however, these very large files will slow down your website and frustrate your site visitors. You should 'compress' your images for website use.

A recommended maximum width guide is 1900 pixels for website page header images.

To do this you can use one of the many photo editing software packages. Some are free and have limited functionality, others charge fees like the popular and powerful **Adobe Photoshop** whichgives you lots ways to be creative with your images and photography.

To automatically reduce image files on a website you can use a plugin, like the free compression software for WordPress called **Smush.**

Tip
Don't worry, when you compress an image file you are reducing the PIXELS not the actual size of the picture.

Ideas and actions...

Shit Happens

Professional training, insurance, cyber security, backup and storage systems – build them into your business BEFORE 'shit' makes its unwanted appearance and ruins your reputation and hard work.

"It's not the shit we face that defines us, it's how we deal with it."

Ahmed Mostafa
Egyptian author, artist, athlete, musician and entrepreneur.

Exclusive Tools and Offers

To support your ideas and ambition I've got some useful resources to help organise your thoughts and information, and keep you on track and on time.

Free Template Library – get organised

Starter Website – get noticed

Translation Support – get talking to the world

Free Template Library
– get organised

I've put together a range of flexible templates that will keep you on top of your scheduling, project hours, invoicing and client contacts.

Fully flexible to be tailored to your business branding and information. Does all the addy ups and take aways. A great way to start as you mean to go on! Use as Microsoft Excel™ documents on your computer or print off and fill in as you wish.

Use the QR code to reveal all your free templates with information and instruction.

Unlimited downloads.

- ✓ Weekly Timesheet
- ✓ Event Marketing Planner
- ✓ Social Media Planner
- ✓ Invoice Template
- ✓ Basic Client Database

Starter Website
– get noticed

Low on cost, big on value.

Start as you mean to go on and begin your business journey with a great website. Together with our partners at The Big Ideas Collective, and drawing and on their extensive web experience, our Web Starter Package will give you a beautiful, professional, reliable and fast website to help you get noticed.

10% OFF a year's hosting using the book code, PLUS, one free email address, and that's not all...

- A choice of fast-loading, responsive and eye-catching designs

- Built-in search engine optimisation (SEO)

- One year's hosting

- Social media integration

- Easy-to-use content editor that lets you update your site anytime, anywhere

- SSL Certificate with leading security features to keep your site safe

- Backup and restore for complete peace of mind

- Data protection guidance for you and your site visitors

- NO hidden costs, slow-loading pages, pop-up adverts (often a feature of cheap hosting packages)

Visit micro-oiseau.com/starter-website-offer/ and quote H2BIBweb10 to get your discount and get started.

Translation Support
– get talking to the world

If you want to talk to the world you need to speak their language.

We have a talented community of translators ready to support you. If you can't see the language you need, just contact us via our website and we can source a translator for you.

Visit micro-oiseau.com/translators/

There is also a practical guide to translation by author and translator Grey Drane. If you're thinking about how to create content in another language, or brief a translation agency, don't miss this great free resource.

Visit micro-oiseau.com/free-translation-guides/

Business Success Means...

1. **Getting to know your competitors**. Just as you should not underestimate your competitors, don't ignore them. They are a valuable resource of knowledge, support, even collaboration. Give kudos for their success. Help them out if you can and the favour is most likely to be returned.

2. **Understanding your skills and carving out a niche**. Knowing what you're really good at doesn't just apply to your products or services, but also your personal skills. If you are not good with numbers, find a bookkeeper. If you are not good at writing, find a copywriter. Maximise what you do well and delegate to others the tasks you do not.

3. **Becoming well known for what you do**. There is nothing more attractive to a customer or supplier than someone who is respected and trusted. Spread your expertise via videos, blogs, eBooks and podcasts – just a few of the ways you can expand your audience and customer reach.

4. **Knowing what it costs**. It is just as important to know what income you need to cover your expenses and make a profit, as it is to identify unnecessary spending. Your accountant or bookkeeper is not in charge of your business, you are. Be and stay in control of your finances.

5. **Surrounding yourself with good people**. Trustworthy, loyal, positive, productive and fun – anything less and you're in for trouble!

6. **Keep listening and learning**. Partners, friends, colleagues, customers, competitors ... sometimes the hardest feedback to hear is the thing that will improve what you do the most.

7. **Following your instincts.** Intuition, 'gut instinct', call it what you like, we have an in-built alert system when it comes to taking chances. If you've got a big decision to make it's important to get the facts, seek advice and listen to what your gut is telling you.

8. **Having values and giving value**. By doing the very best you can your team will respect you, your customers will return and your business will grow.

"You have brains in your head. You have feet in your shoes. You can steer yourself any direction you choose."

Dr. Seuss
Theodor Suess Geisel, American children's author and cartoonist.

For more articles and useful stuff, including free business templates, visit www.micro-oiseau.com.

Ideas and actions...

Further Reading

How to Get Inside Someone's Mind and Stay There, by Jacky Fitt, Business Expert Press, ISBN 9781948198455

Winner 2015 Small Business Book Awards Marketing
"An absolute gem."
"... full of intelligent insights and common sense advice."
"Unlocks the mystery of good marketing and communications."

In 2015 my first book, *How to Get Inside Someone's Mind and Stay There* won the Small Business Book Marketing Award in the US. Looking at content marketing and production of well-written content.

I have mentioned several books and resources throughout the text. I've noted them here, along with others that I have found useful and inspirational.

Creative Mischief by Dave Trott, LOAF Marketing Ltd, ISBN: 9780956435705

ethicability by Professor Roger Steare, The Big Ideas Library, ISBN: 9780955236952

Fear Less by Pippa Grange, Ebury Publishing, ISBN: 9781785042928

How to Do What's Right by Professor Roger Steare, free eBook https://thecorporatephilosopher.org/book/

How to Win Friends and Influence People by Dale Carnegie, Ebury Publishing, ISBN: 9780091906818

I Am Human. 30 Mistakes to Success by Martin Johnson, The Big Ideas Library, ISBN: 9780992985981

Mass Persuasion Method by Bushra Azhar, Best Seller Publishing, ISBN: 1946978108

Start with Why by Simon Sinek, Penguin Books Ltd, ISBN: 9780241958223

The Power of Regret by Daniel H. Pink, Canongate Books, ISBN: 9781838857066

Toxic Positivity by Whitney Goodman, Orion Publishing, ISBN: 9781398704879

Write to Sell by Andy Maslen, Marshall Cavendish International, 3rd Ed. ISBN: 9789814868235

Last, but by no means least, why not discover your MoralDNA®?

Take the free Moral DNA test, because doing the right thing isn't always easy, yet understanding how we make up our minds means we're more likely to do the right thing, in the right way, more of the time.

Visit https://moraldna.org

Acknowledgements

If it takes a village to raise a child, then it takes just as many people to produce a book.

At the beginning of my book I introduced you to Ned Hoste, my friend and business partner. We have worked together for many years and, rather strangely, can't remember how we met. Thanks to Ned for a shopping list of 'must-haves' for a great collaborator, including the patience of a saint, honesty, creative genius and unflappable humour. All the bird cartoons have been created by Ned as a sideline to his book design, publishing and web mastery. Astonishing.

Thanks to my family. They live the production of any creative work with you and I'm very blessed with a wonderful husband Thomas and two of the most inspiring people I know, my daughters Phoebe and Esmée. Their support is fantastic and unwavering.

To those who have supplied me with thoughtful feedback and words of wisdom, I am endebted to Roger Steare, Jo Clarke, Chris Hiscocks, Martin Johnson, Jackie Mathers, Todd Hannula, Dawn O'Keefe, Anj Handa, Andy Lock and for the proofreading skills of Marcus Parry, thank you all for your time, expertise and support. From my clients to my dance class, and Sue and Sarah at the Afternoon Art Club; time out is just as important as the time on the job, balance makes us better at everything.

Micro Oiseau is a web based project that began in 2020 to offer free marketing advice in as many languages as possible. This book is part of that wider project, which continues today. To my community of translators who responded to Micro Oiseau a very big thank you. The kindness of strangers is wonderful, as is their trust, enthusiasm and generosity. Thanks also to those who have asked me to talk to groups and students taking their first steps in business. I learn so much from them, we're all works in progress.

Most importantly, thank you for reading this book. I raise my favourite tea mug to your enterprise and shaping the successful business and fulfilling life you're looking for. I'm delighted that this book may be able to play a useful part in your journey. With hard work and sound advice, you'll make it!

© Colin McLean

Initially working in theatre, film and TV, Jacky Fitt is a highly successful copywriter and award-winning author. Recognised for her approachable and accessible style, Jacky's first book on content marketing won the Small Business Book for Marketing in the US. A writer of articles, blogs and websites, non-fiction editor and TEDx speaker, Jacky is also co-founder of The Big Ideas Collective creative agency. Born in London, Jacky has lived in York for many years with her family and is a Fellow of the Royal Society for the encouragement of Arts, Manufactures and Commerce. A keen promoter of business startup help for everyone, everywhere, Jacky's multi-lingual project Micro Oiseau showcases new translators, as well as free marketing support.